Gregory's Girl

THE FILMSCRIPT

by **Bill Forsyth**

Editor **Paul Kelley**

The Television Literacy Project

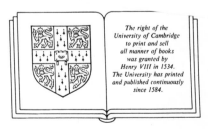

The right of the
University of Cambridge
to print and sell
all manner of books
was granted by
Henry VIII in 1534.
The University has printed
and published continuously
since 1584.

CAMBRIDGE UNIVERSITY PRESS
Cambridge
New York   Port Chester   Melbourne   Sydı

Published by the Press Syndicate of the University of Cambridge
The Pitt Building, Trumpington Street, Cambridge CB2 1RP
40 West 20th Street, New York, NY 10011, USA
10 Stamford Road, Oakleigh, Melbourne 3166, Australia

First published 1991

Printed in Great Britain at the University Press, Cambridge

British Library cataloguing in publication data

Forsyth, Bill
Gregory's girl filmscript.
1. British cinema films – Scripts
I. Title
791.4372

ISBN 0 521 38838 4

The front cover shows a scene from the film, with John Gordon-Sinclair as Gregory and Dee Hepburn as Dorothy. (Photograph by Tom Hilton.)

GO

ey

Contents

Introduction

There is no doubt that *Gregory's Girl* is one of the most striking films about young people made in the 1980s. From shortly after its release, the film has come to be regarded as one of the classics of its time. It is worth while looking briefly at why this is so.

On the surface the film might be popular because it deals with the relationship between the sexes. It manages to look at the relationships between teenagers without being overly romantic or too cynical. Gregory himself is an appealing figure, not because he is particularly handsome, brave or intelligent, but because he cares and can be hurt, and yet retains his sense of humour. Many people can recognise something of themselves in Gregory, and in his situation. And *Gregory's Girl* shows us his problems in a direct way that makes perfectly clear the embarrassment he (and we?) feel. Even in the moments of farce – when Gregory covers up his nipples with his fingers, for example – it is possible to have some sympathy for him, and for all of the people who find the transition into adult life difficult.

On a more serious level, the film seems to challenge some of society's assumptions about women. Although there is the character of Steve who is the expert cook, it is Dorothy herself – and her skill at football – who seems to raise the question of women's rights most directly. The very fact that Dorothy is good at football makes us look again at our assumptions about sport and women. And if we take the film seriously – and it is possible to do so – then it is depressing to see that ten years after its release it is still forbidden for girls to participate in mixed-sex football in school (or out). The kind of open-minded approach to skilful football players that is assumed in the film doesn't yet exist.

But *Gregory's Girl* is not popular because it deals with relationships and the role of women. There is something about the feel of the film – its tone if you like – that is very attractive. Perhaps this feeling is inspired by Gregory himself, with his combination of innocence and the desire to know, the knack of making himself look a fool and not caring. This feeling that the film has is also reflected in the kind of humour it has: many of the scenes have a humour that arises from one character's ability to see the excesses of another as funny. In this way it is something of a satire on the follies of the young, but one that sees great virtues in the young as well; there are no really evil characters.

Having written all this it seems to me that there is much more to the film than these rather general points. A film is visual. It is not the character or the words of the script that really matter: it is what you see and hear on the screen. And like other films (and television), the complex of meanings made up from pictures and sound is the real source of the success of *Gregory's Girl*. Therefore the impact of the film can best be appreciated in a cinema. This script is only an aid to help those who wish to consider the film in more detail.

Pre-production and post-production

The script that is printed here is the post-production script. This is the script written after the film was completed, and one that records more or less exactly what the characters say and do in the film. In many ways it is very different from the pre-production script (the author's version before filming began). Obviously changes may have to be made in a script during shooting, or because a particular piece of film didn't come out. Sometimes a script is altered for other reasons.

In the Appendix a number of the earlier versions of the film are set out, and these come from the pre-production script. One of the most interesting is the old opening of the film, which was much quieter, and concentrated on football rather than on voyeurs. It is interesting to consider why some of these scenes were left out (and many others were placed in a different order), and they do shed further light on the author's original plans for the film. A study of these may also help people to understand something of the very fluid nature of some film scripts: scripts are not sacred, even when the author is also the director (as Bill Forsyth was). What is certain is that the final film is not fluid: what was finally assembled was the only final version. And it is this version – a collective work by the many people listed here as Cast and Credits – that should be the real area of interest.

Paul Kelley

Acknowledgements

The makers of *Gregory's Girl* gratefully thank:

The pupils and staff of Abronhill High School
Cumbernauld Development Corporation
Scottish Film Council
Partick Thistle Football Club
Umbro International
JLG Ltd
Budget Rent-A-Car
Woolco
Strathclyde Regional Council Education Department
Suzy Potter of Wavelength
John Baraldi
Cumbernauld Theatre
Liz Lochhead
Mercedes McGum
Alan Pattillo

Gregory's Girl was completed in 1980. Below are the credits and cast of the film.

Credits

Camera Operator	Jan Pester
1st Assistant Director	Ian Madden
2nd Assistant Director	Terry Dalzell
Continuity	Anne Coulter
Art Director	Adrienne Atkinson
Wardrobe	Nadia Arthur
Make-up	Lois Burwell
Sound Mixer	Louis Kramer
Dubbing Mixer	Tony Anscombe
Electrics	Alex Mackenzie Lighting
Focus Puller	Lewis Foster
Clapper/Loader	Norman Halley
Boom Operator	Cameron Crosby
Sound Assistant	Alan Brerton
Grip	Allan Ross
Assistant Editor	Fiona Macdonald
Unit Publicist	Geoff Freeman
Stills Photographer	Tom Hilton
Assistant Art Directors	Gus Maclean
	Ross Balfour
2nd Assistant Editor	Sitar Rose
Production Accountant	Louise Coulter
Production Assistant	Margaret Waldie
Producer's Secretary	Christine Higgs
Unit Runners	David Brown
	John Hardy
	David Ferguson
	Eric Coulter
Football Coach	Donnie McKinnon
Music	Colin Tully
Director of Photography	Michael Coutler
Editor	John Gow
Production Supervisor	Paddy Higson
Producers	Davina Belling
	Clive Parsons
Written and Directed by	Bill Forsyth

Cast

Gregory	John Gordon-Sinclair
Dorothy	Dee Hepburn
Phil Menzies	Jake D'Arcy
Susan	Clare Grogan
Andy	Robert Buchanan
Steve	William Greenlees
Eric	Alan Love
Carol	Caroline Guthrie
Margo	Carol Macartney
Billy	Douglas Sannachan
Madeline	Allison Forster
Head	Chic Murray
Alec	Alex Norton
Alistair	John Bett
Gregory's Father	David Anderson
Mr Anderson	Billy Feeley
Miss Ford	Maeve Watt
Miss Welch	Muriel Romanes
Mr Hall	Patrick Lewsley
Alan	Ronald Girvin
Kelvin	Pat Harkins
Gordon	Tony Whitmore
Richard	Denis Griman
Charlie	Graham Thompson
Brenda	Natasha Gerson
Penguin	Christopher Higson
Football Teams	Our Lady's High School
	Greenfaulds High School
	Cumbernauld High School

Gregory's Girl

1   Exterior. Nurses' Hostel. Night.   1

We see the other boys – ANDY, CHARLIE, ERIC and PETE –
before we see GREGORY. There is a feeling of excitement in
the air. The boys talk in forced whispers – for no real reason,
because they are quite a distance from 'the action'.

We climax their excited mixture of voices by revealing more
and more of the show at a nurse's window.

ERIC   Where? Where is it?

ANDY   In the middle. There . . . there.

BOY   Yeah, I've got it. I've got it.

ERIC   Oh yes. Yes.

1ST BOY   (*out of view*) Look at that!

2ND BOY   (*out of view*) Calm down. I can't concentrate.

GREGORY   Oh, that's a brassière. She's got a brassière.

ERIC   Take it off – take it off.

ANDY   Transmit. Tell her to take off her bra.

ERIC   Take off your brassière.

ANDY   Concentrate, you bastards. Concentrate!

By now we are intercutting eagerly between the faces and the
action in the window.

One of the boys, ANDY, is affected rather dramatically by
what he is seeing. He finds it difficult to breathe, he gasps for

air and seems to rock on his feet, as if his heartbeat has accelerated to maximum revs.

>ANDY I . . . I . . . I can't breathe.

The other BOYS are obliged to give ANDY some of their attention, although they do so reluctantly. They offer him support whilst keeping their eyes fixed on the nurse.

>GREGORY Oh Andy . . . grow up!

>ANDY I . . . I . . . I can't see right.

The BOYS now look around them anxiously, conscious about the disturbance ANDY is causing. To tell the truth, they have *all* been moved more than somewhat by their experience.

Collectively, they decide to move off into the shadows to recover their wits. They half-drag ANDY with them, all of them with their attention still fixed on the window as they move back into the darkness.

>PETE God, Eric, where's your camera? What a picture! What a photograph!

>ERIC I could make a fortune with a photograph like that!

>PETE What a doll! What a doll!

>ANDY That was terrific! Superb. What are we doing tomorrow night?

>ERIC Coming back.

>ANDY Aye, you're right. We could bring some sandwiches.

We are still intercutting between the NURSE at the window and the retreating BOYS. As they disappear into the darkness two smaller FIGURES emerge from the cover of a shrub.

They are about ten years old, and look like brothers. They are cool and calm, although they give the window just as much attention as the older boys. One of them glances in the direction of the departed gang.

    1ST BOY   A lot of fuss over a bit of tit, eh?

The other boy still has his attention fixed on the window,
although minus the fuss of GREGORY and company.

    2ND BOY Yeah. Hey, look, the knickers.

    1ST BOY Oh yeah.

We end the scene with a final look at the view in the window,
and the very composed faces of the young BOYS.

2   Ext. Countryside. Day.   2

DOROTHY is running on the grass, training.

3   Ext. Football Ground. Day.   3

We begin as the REFEREE blows his whistle to end the match.
From the faces and reactions of the PLAYERS as they leave the
field it's obvious that some are winners and some are losers.
Even in the simple business of leaving the field and heading
for the dressing room, OUR TEAM manage to demonstrate
some of their ineptness. ANDY the goalkeeper drops the ball
he is carrying, fumbles to catch it, misses, and has to chase it
between the legs of the others. One boy is reacting with a fit
of mild hysterics. He is GREGORY. He is leaving the field in a
fit of laughter, shaking his head, laughing some more. Weak
with laughter, he supports himself on the shoulder of one of
his team mates. During the whole scene the sad – so sad that
it's almost devoid of expression – face of PHIL MENZIES, the
Gym Teacher and Team Coach, watches from the sideline.

4   Interior. Dressing Room. Day.   4

A few minutes have passed, and GREGORY is now almost
alone in the dressing room, changing into school uniform, or

his version of it. During the ensuing dialogue he continues changing, the business of this adding to the scene where it can: such things as GREGORY applying his roll-on deodorant, putting in his earring, and putting on his neck-chain. PHIL MENZIES joins him.

GREGORY has retained his good humour from the previous scene.

ANDY See you, Gregory.

GREGORY (*almost laughing*) Terrible game, eh?

PHIL Bad, very bad.

GREGORY Yeah. You've got to laugh.

PHIL And what have you got to laugh about?

GREGORY Us. (*He senses a hurt in PHIL. He tries to make amends.*) Football is all about entertainment. We give them a good laugh. It's only a game.

PHIL It's only a game. It's only *eight* games. Eight games in a row you've lost.

GREGORY Can't lose them all. You push us really hard, no mercy, lots of discipline. Get tough.

PHIL We need *goals*. It's your job to get them and you don't.

GREGORY Well, nobody's perfect. It's a tricky time for me. Doing a lot of growing. It slows you down. Five inches this year. (*He crouches down so that he's level with PHIL, and their faces are very close together.*) Remember last year I was only down here. (*GREGORY is crouching and staring into PHIL's face.*) Are you growing a moustache?

PHIL I want to make some changes.

GREGORY Good idea. It'll make you look older.

PHIL   In the team. I want to make some changes in the team.

GREGORY   You're the boss.

PHIL   I want to try out some other people.

GREGORY   Switch the team around?

PHIL   Take some people out. I was going to take you out.

GREGORY   You don't want to do that.

GREGORY by now is applying his underarm deodorant.

PHIL   Yes I do.

GREGORY   You don't.

PHIL   I do.

GREGORY   (*pauses and changes armpit*) You don't. (*PHIL is silent.*) What about Andy? He's not even *started* growing yet. He's going to be in *real* trouble. (*PHIL is thinking.*) I'll tell him.

PHIL   I'll tell him. A week's trial in goal for you. Then I'll decide.

GREGORY   Have you got a jersey my size? Andy's a lot smaller.

PHIL   Never mind about the jersey. A week's trial, then I decide.

GREGORY   You're the boss. Who's taking over my position?

PHIL   I want to try out some new people.

GREGORY is dressed now and ready to leave. He makes his way to the door.

GREGORY   You won't regret this.

PHIL's face has adopted that same sad non-expression that he wore on the football field. If it says anything then it says that he is already regretting 'this'.

GREGORY leaves the room and we follow him as he makes his way down the corridor. He mimes a couple of football passes to himself, like a boxer shadow boxing. PHIL, still in the dressing room, opens the door and looks down the corridor after him. GREGORY by some irritating coincidence looks back and catches PHIL watching him. PHIL dodges back into the dressing room and is alone.

Fade out.

5   Ext. Motorway Bridge. Day.   5

GREGORY and ANDY are walking across a motorway bridge.

GREGORY   OK, so Phil Menzies is daft. He's daft enough maybe to square out the team. I'm not saying he will fling out – no, I didn't say that – but he's daft enough to do it. Look, I'll tell you what, I'll tell you what – if, just supposing Phil Menzies is daft enough to throw you out the team – well, I'll resign.

ANDY   Really?

GREGORY   Yeah, well when I – when I say 'resign' what I'm getting at – what it boils down to – what I'm trying to say really is – I'll resign myself to making a decision, if it happens. I'm not saying that it will – it might – but it won't, I don't think so.

ANDY   Well, I'll see you later Gregory, OK?

GREGORY   Oh, where are you going?

ANDY   Oh, I just want to stay here a wee bit longer and watch the traffic. I like looking at the big trucks.

GREGORY Huh.

    ANDY Look, do you know that at least twelve tons
         of cornflakes passes under here every day?

GREGORY Really?

    ANDY It's a well-known fact.

GREGORY Huh, gee, is it? I never knew that.

    ANDY I'll see you later.

GREGORY Yes, see you.

GREGORY heads off and ANDY stays on the bridge.

6   Ext. Town/School. Day.   6

BOYS are walking, carrying school bags, cases, and so on.
ANDY and GREGORY are among them.

    GREGORY Had that dream again last night. Oh, it was
         terrific!

Part of the journey to school takes some girls past a
MOTORWAY GANG, who are setting to work on a grassy
verge by the walkway. They give the girls appreciative looks
and gestures, as they lean on their hoes and brushes.

7   Int. School. Day.   7

We quickly establish the feeling of the school settling down
for the day's work. The stairways and corridors gradually
empty of people.

Then we hear the sound of solitary light footsteps in the
corridor, and we cut to find SUSAN making her way to her
class. She is late and slightly flustered. Her hair is
disarranged, and she seems to have too many things to carry.
We follow her up the stairs and along the corridor. She stops

at a classroom door. She doesn't go in right away. She fixes her blouse and her skirt and her hair. Then she goes in, and the school is settled again.

8   Int. Gregory's Bedroom. Day.   8

We see GREGORY as he opens his eyes. He takes a second or two to come awake. Then he suddenly sits up in bed and stares ahead of him to the foot of the bed. When he sees his reflection in the mirror on the wardrobe door he seems comforted. He relaxes and lies back on the pillow again. But only for a second. He checks the time on his watch and quickly gets out of bed.

He is just about to take off his pyjama top when he notices the open curtains at the window. With the curtains closed he seems more at ease as he dresses.

He moves to his drums and starts to play them. He stops.

9   Int. Gregory's Kitchen. Day.   9

He prepares his breakfast: a not very elaborate affair, mostly things squeezed out of tubes and scraped out of cans. There are lots of gadgets around the kitchen, labour-savers for the modern working family. GREGORY seems adept with all of them, including the coffee-making machine, which hisses and bubbles and obviously needs a lot of skilled attention.

GREGORY demonstrates his expertise with the electric toothbrush. He leaves it on the side as he starts breakfast.

GREGORY takes some money from underneath a plant pot.

10   Ext. Gregory's House. Day.   10

GREGORY leaves his house and makes his way down the cul-de-sac. The New Town feeling is very evident, with

pre-school kids all over the place. Some of them greet
GREGORY as he makes his way past them.

Another young voice greets him, and we see a three-year-old
girl sitting up a tree on an area of lawn. She is in fact perched
on the supporting post of a sapling much too light to take her
weight. How she got up there is a total mystery.

11   Int. Gregory's Kitchen. Day.   11

The toothbrush is still on.

12   Int./Ext. Car/Road. Day.   12

A driving lesson is in progress. We film from the rear seat of
the car, and have the INSTRUCTOR, the PUPIL, and the
forward view in shot. The INSTRUCTOR is GREGORY'S
FATHER.

The car is gingerly negotiating a roundabout.

> FATHER   Two advantages about learning to drive in
>   this New Town environment – very obvious
>   ones – up into third here.

He speaks in the measured, rational tones of the professional
instructor.

> FATHER   The absence of traffic lights. Total absence of
>   stray pedestrians. But you must remember
>   that in other towns things won't be so
>   controlled.

Through the windscreen a figure appears, walking briskly
down the road, oblivious of traffic hazards. This of course is
GREGORY. When GREGORY eventually becomes aware of the
car he doesn't make a rational attempt to get out of its way:
he simply lets it chase him down the middle of the road.

The forced calmness in the INSTRUCTOR's voice only serves

to accentuate the sense of imminent disaster.

> FATHER Mirror and brake! That's the way. Relax
> position. Brake! That's the way.

The car comes to rest with GREGORY just about to straddle
the bonnet. The engine stalls. GREGORY goes into a very
dumb routine, pretending that nothing has happened, that
the car and his FATHER are in fact not there, that he is still on
his very normal way to school. He is just about to walk off
when his FATHER calls him.

> FATHER Come here you!

> PUPIL Is that the emergency stop?

> FATHER Emergency stop, unsimulated, yes.

GREGORY by now has admitted the existence of the car, and
his FATHER, and the incident. He makes his way to his old
man's window. He smiles.

> GREGORY Hi Mike.

> FATHER Call me 'Dad', Gregory, or 'Pop', or
> something. It makes me feel better when you
> call me 'Dad' or 'Father'.

> GREGORY Listen, I won't take up any more of your
> time. I know what it's like when you're
> driving under instruction.

> PUPIL That was my first emergency stop, by the
> way.

> GREGORY Was it? Oh, it was very good – very good
> that. Yeah.

FATHER overrides this appeal to the PUPIL.

> FATHER Stay, Gregory! (*Then, in a calmer voice*) I'm
> sure Mr Clark would like a minute or two to
> collect his thoughts anyway.

> PUPIL My name's Anderson.

FATHER   Oh. What's the score? Are you going to
          school late or going home early? (*Then to the
          PUPIL*) Handbrake and neutral, Mr Clark.

GREGORY's technique with his FATHER seems to involve a
total avoidance of verbal commitment to anything, plus
smiling a lot. He smiles now, and ignores his FATHER's
question. Behind it all, though, we can sense a basic warmth
between them, and his FATHER isn't short of a wry twist of
humour.

GREGORY   How are you anyway?

FATHER   Oh fine, we're all very well. Your mother –
          you remember your mother?

GREGORY   Yeah, I remember Mum.

FATHER   She was asking about you just the other day.
          I told her that we had met briefly in the
          hallway last Thursday and you looked fine.

GREGORY takes this with an awkward smile. In the
background the PUPIL is in a world of his own, hanging onto
the steering wheel, negotiating imaginary hairpin bends in
some Monte Carlo rally of the mind.

FATHER   Listen, I've got an idea: why don't we meet
          up for breakfast some time later in the week.
          Say, eight o'clock in the kitchen, Friday?

GREGORY is trapped into treating this as a serious social
request. He nods and smiles again.

GREGORY   Yeah. Yeah, sounds fine. Yeah.

FATHER   It's a date then.

GREGORY   Yeah.

FATHER   Ignition, mirror, signal, gear.

The PUPIL comes back to reality and restarts the car. They
start to move off. FATHER shouts a final word to GREGORY.

19

> FATHER And we'll start the driving lessons as soon as
> you've mastered the walking bit, OK?

GREGORY watches the car lurch its way round the corner,
and then continues on his way to school.

13   Int. Staffroom. Day.   13

We begin with a *point-of-view* shot from the window,
looking down into the school yard. GREGORY is approaching
the school and is making too much of an effort to look casual
and not late. He makes abrupt and manic-looking changes of
direction, heading for one entrance and then suddenly
bolting for another. We hear the first few lines of dialogue
over his antics.

> ALEC Every bloody morning.

> ALISTAIR He's mad. He should be locked up.

When we cut to the room interior we find ALEC and ALISTAIR
at the window, and PHIL just about to enter the room. PHIL
hovers at the door for a bit. The others haven't noticed him
and so he tries to announce it.

> PHIL Any tea?

They go on ignoring him and looking out of the window.

> ALEC Bloody bastard.

> ALISTAIR He must think he's invisible.

PHIL vaguely wonders if they are talking about him.

> ALEC Stupid bastard.

PHIL's curiosity takes him to the window to join them.

> PHIL Who is it?

ALEC and ALISTAIR turn and walk away from the window.

> ALEC It's that daft boy in fourth year. The one

> that's in your football team. Well, I heard
> they were awarded a corner last week and
> did a lap of honour . . .

PHIL ignores the joke, and frowns with realisation when he works out that they are talking about GREGORY.

> PHIL   Oh him. His days are numbered. After next
> week he's out! Kaput, finished. I'm going to
> get some new blood in the team. Big
> changes.

PHIL is getting quietly worked up.

> ALISTAIR   Yeah, have a sponge cake Phil.

PHIL accepts one from the plate, and talks on.

> PHIL   A new regime. Signing a new striker this
> morning. (*He gives the cake a suspicious look.*)
> Er, er, who made these?

> ALEC   Relax. It was Sandra and Alice in 3A. Very
> nice girls, very clean.

PHIL gives an uncharacteristic smile.

> PHIL   Oh Sandra and Alice, eh? Very nice girls, eh
> Alistair? Still getting the poems from wee
> June as well eh? You'll get put away.

PHIL seems very pleased with himself and the rough male banter he has instigated. ALISTAIR and ALEC are unmoved.

> ALISTAIR   I like your moustache.

> PHIL   Does it show already? I've only been
> growing it two days. Thanks a lot.

> ALEC   It's really nice. It makes you look very grown-
> up.

> PHIL   Thanks.

> ALISTAIR   Very mature.

> ALEC Yeah. You're right. I mean you look at least
> fifteen already.

PHIL retreats in a very businesslike manner.

> PHIL Well, I've got to scram. I've got an important
> morning this morning. One place in the team
> for the best striker. I've organised a trial – see
> what they're like under pressure. I'll see you
> later.

ALISTAIR and ALEC allow PHIL to ramble on, watching him
coolly. PHIL exits, and they exchange a smile. ALEC gets
serious first.

> ALEC *Are* you still getting the poems from June?

ALISTAIR gets mildly edgy, but it's half a joke.

> ALISTAIR Oh come on, you know it's not right to ask
> those sorts of questions. We're dealing with
> the emotions of a vulnerable, sensitive,
> sixteen-year-old redhead.

14 Int. School Corridor. Day. 14

PHIL is making his way briskly to the Gym. Of all the two
thousand souls in the school he has to encounter GREGORY.
There is no way they can avoid each other in the corridor, so
PHIL accelerates his pace somewhat and eases the
awkwardness as they pass with a few words.

> PHIL Oh, might have some news for you by
> lunchtime son. I'll keep you posted.

GREGORY stares after him, intrigued. So intrigued that after a
few paces and a moment of thought, he retraces his steps and
follows PHIL's route to the Gym.

PHIL is assembling his half-dozen hopefuls for the trial
session: six BOYS in assorted football gear. PHIL is handing
out a football to each of them, and explaining the procedure.

> PHIL   Right. You all know what I'm looking for – a
> goal scorer. That requires two basic skills:
> ball control, shooting accuracy and the
> ability to *read the game* . . . three things.

The boys look on attentively, as if they actually understand
what PHIL is going on about.

> PHIL   So this trial will allow me to assess these two
> – three – basic aspects of your skills. Right?
> (*He notices one boy's feet.*) What's the idea of
> sandshoes, boy? Have you no boots?

The BOY shakes his head.

> BOY   I'll get some if I get the place.

> PHIL   No, that's a dead loss, son. Go and get
> changed. We play in real boots in this school,
> from the word go.

The BOY wanders off to the school building as PHIL talks on.

> PHIL   Right. Basic ball control. Trotting with the
> ball at your feet, fifty yards and back. Two
> lines. Come on, go!

As the dismissed BOY is reaching the building, another
figure is emerging, dressed in a dark tracksuit. We intercut
between the action with PHIL and the boys, and the
approaching figure. Soon the figure is discernibly female,
and blonde. It is of course DOROTHY.

> PHIL   Both sides of the foot! Now, come on, I want
> to see complete control!

DOROTHY approaches the group. PHIL presumes that she is

on some errand or other and gives her little attention.

> PHIL Come on – faster now. (*A half-glance to DOROTHY*.) Come on, a little more pace, anybody can *walk* with a ball. Come on. Well, what d'you want lass? Faster now!

DOROTHY stands beside PHIL and waits for his attention. She is very cool and self-contained. PHIL soon gets the vibes of her presence.

> PHIL What do you want, dear?

> DOROTHY I'm here for the trial.

PHIL doesn't allow himself to comprehend. He backs off into a slightly patronising tone.

> PHIL Look, this is a football trial dear. Maybe Miss McAlpine's up to something with the hockey team, I don't know, but this here is football, for boys.

> DOROTHY That's right, football trials – eleven a.m. – I saw the notice.

PHIL gives a laugh, trying to stay in control of things.

> PHIL Look, I'm sorry you picked it up wrongly, dear, but it was boys I wanted for the trials.

> DOROTHY It didn't say so on the notice. Just said 'talented players'.

DOROTHY is holding her ground firmly. PHIL tries getting tougher.

> PHIL There's been a slight misunderstanding, obviously, but there's nothing I can do about it now. Come on!

PHIL seems prepared to let the matter end there. He lets his attention drift back to the BOYS, who by now are beginning to drift round PHIL and DOROTHY. DOROTHY puts some more pressure on.

> DOROTHY You didn't say 'boys only'. You're not allowed to anyway. I want a trial.

PHIL knows he is losing ground.

> PHIL It's not possible, dear – not today – we don't have a spare ball.

DOROTHY nods towards the ball that the departed BOY has left. She moves for it and with the gentlest of flicks of her foot raises the ball from the ground and seems to float it into her hands.

> DOROTHY Here's one.

DOROTHY and PHIL face each other. The challenge is open now. PHIL gives in.

DOROTHY joins one of the lines and does her stuff. She moves with the ball as if it was anchored to her feet with elastic. She still keeps half an eye on PHIL, and he certainly keeps an eye on her.

None of the boys can match DOROTHY's skill in even this simple exercise.

We see GREGORY, who has followed PHIL here and witnessed the events so far. GREGORY has an expression that reveals definite interest in what is going on, and very possible interest in Dorothy. We see on his face his awakening interest in DOROTHY. Just wait until she gets the tracksuit off. PHIL is still irritated by DOROTHY, but he is also impressed by her. They move on to another exercise.

> PHIL OK, into twos now. I want to see some penetration work and a shot for goal. One attacker, one defender. It's an open goal, so let's see who's first to score.

> DOROTHY Right, you defend me.

There's not really much question about whose ball will be first in the net. The six hopefuls line themselves up in three pairs. DOROTHY is one of the attacking three. They start off, and the three defenders come out for them. We cut quickly between DOROTHY's action and the faces of PHIL and GREGORY. Her ball rips into the net.

> CHARLIE What's going on?

> GREGORY She's gorgeous. She is absolutely gorgeous.

> ANDY It's Dorothy.

The other BOYS are bewildered. They look to PHIL for some leadership.

> PHIL Do it again. Same pairs.

> CHARLIE She's got funny ears!

The same thing happens again. PHIL gets tougher.

> PHIL Right. Three shots each at goal now. Let's see how you do against a real goalkeeper.

PHIL himself goes into the goal. The BOYS and DOROTHY form a line for three shots each at the goal.

> PHIL You first dear?

Three times we cut back to the goal mouth, and three times we see DOROTHY hammer the ball past PHIL into the net. PHIL just saves the last shot from one of the boys. The trial seems to be over.

> PHIL Right, that's it. Finished. Stamina test – once round the playing fields and back to the dressing room. It's only quarter of a mile and should be treated as a sprint. Off you go.

The five BOYS and DOROTHY race off round the field. PHIL turns his back on them, and heads for the building.

We watch the progress of the race. DOROTHY is in the lead already, pulling ahead of the bunch at the second corner.

DOROTHY is finishing well in front of the rest. She runs up to a halt beside PHIL, and she is hardly out of breath.

>> DOROTHY Well?

PHIL has no time to be patronising now.

>> PHIL I'll let everyone know in the fullness of time. I'll pass the word to Miss McAlpine.

DOROTHY gets very forceful.

>> DOROTHY I was the best! You *know* I was the best!

As if to help her make her point, the BOYS are straggling in off the field now, sweating and panting.

>> PHIL It's not that simple. It could be out of my hands. We'll have to see.

>> DOROTHY If I was the best I should be in the team. The notice said so.

>> PHIL I said we'll see. You might very well get into the team.

PHIL moves off for his office. DOROTHY follows him.

>> DOROTHY You've got to put me on the team list. I want to sign something.

The two of them hurry past GREGORY and the other two.

>> GREGORY What a dream.

>> DOROTHY Mr Menzies. I want to sign something. Mr Menzies, open the door!

Outside, ANDY speaks to CHARLIE.

>> ANDY Look Charlie, we've got to get some girls. We've got to make a move. Even Gregory's at

it now. We're falling behind. I don't think there's any advantage in putting it off any longer. Besides, it's making me depressed.

16   Int. Cookery Class. Day.   16

The class is under way and GREGORY comes in late. The pupils, in groups of two to an oven, are mixing and rolling out dough and studying menus. GREGORY briskly moves through the class, taking off his jacket and rolling up his shirt sleeves as he goes. He arrives at his cooker, where his friend STEVE is already working. GREGORY mimes a kind of 'sorry I'm late' routine, and puts on his apron. STEVE is an expert cook. GREGORY is his help. GREGORY tries to give the impression of being eager to make himself useful. The first thing he does is hold out his hands for STEVE's inspection. It's a ritual.

> STEVE   Hands?

GREGORY indicates a small mark on one palm.

> GREGORY   That's just paint there.

> STEVE   I've got the biscuit mix started, you go and put the oven on 450 degrees.

> GREGORY   Yes, boss.

A girl, ANNE, has left her own work area and approaches STEVE. He's the acknowledged expert cooking-wise. ANNE is wearing a worried look and a grotty apron. The joy of the Culinary Art is a firmly closed book to her.

> ANNE   Steve, can you help me out with this pastry mix thing?

> STEVE   Pastry mix? There's more than one kind, you know. Short crust, flaky, rough puff?

> ANNE   Well, Margaret's doing the Strudel Soup, and I'm doing the pie. It's the eggs I'm not sure of.

STEVE   Strudel Soup? I'd love to try some of that. It's noodle soup, and don't put eggs in the pastry anyway. It's eight ounces of flour, four ounces of margarine . . .

GREGORY   A pinch of salt.

STEVE   Mix it up, put it into the oven for fifteen minutes. That's it. No eggs, no strudels, nothing – OK?

ANNE has got the message but is not impressed.

ANNE   That's *simple*, really easy.

She wanders off.

STEVE   OK? There, these are five guys in fifth year crying themselves to sleep over that.

GREGORY   Six if you count the music teacher.

STEVE stops GREGORY mixing.

STEVE   Take it easy, just take it easy.

GREGORY   Have you ever been in love? I'm in love.

GREGORY means it. He is abstractly stirring the sponge mix with his finger. This more than anything makes STEVE take notice.

STEVE   Since when?

GREGORY   Half an hour ago. It's great. I'm so restless and I'm dizzy. It's wonderful. Bet I don't get any sleep tonight.

STEVE   That sounds more like indigestion.

GREGORY   No, I'm serious.

STEVE   Who is it? Is it a mature woman? Did you wash your hands?

GREGORY   Don't be crude. It's someone in the football team.

STEVE is silent for a moment.

> STEVE   Really?

> GREGORY   Yeah.

> STEVE   Have you told anyone else about this? It's probably just a phase. Who is it – Andy?

> GREGORY   It's not – it's Dorothy. She's a girl.

> STEVE   Oh.

GREGORY is getting carried away.

> GREGORY   She's got lovely long hair. And she smells mmmm, really gorgeous. Even if you just walk past her in the corridor she smells gorgeous. She's got teeth, lovely white teeth, lovely white white teeth.

> STEVE   Oh, *that* Dorothy – the hair, the teeth and the smell. *That* Dorothy. And she's in the team?

> GREGORY   Well, I think she's taking my position. Well, she's a very good footballer.

> STEVE   Can she cook? Can she do this?

STEVE throws his rolled-out pastry into the air and juggles it with a pizza-maker's flourish.

> GREGORY   Look, Steve, when you're in love, things like that just don't matter.

> STEVE   Gimme the margarine.

> GREGORY   Think she'll love me back?

> STEVE   No chance. Watch that mix. It'll go stiff.

STEVE takes GREGORY's hands in his and guides him through the movements of a nice and easy stir.

> GREGORY   What d'you mean, 'no chance'?

> STEVE   No chance.

17   Ext. Playing Field/Countryside. Day.   17

GREGORY and DOROTHY: intercut shots of them, bringing them together for at least once in the film; shots of DOROTHY in her tracksuit, going through her training routine with care and effort; shots of GREGORY jogging and puffing his way through his own training; shots of GREGORY saving some more brilliant goals at his mirror in his pyjamas. It can't be helped that she'll be nicer to watch, a better footballer, more dedicated in her training, because she is. GREGORY is a lover though, so he belongs in the scene with her.

18   Ext. Football Field. Day.   18

During the early part of this scene another ingredient will be occasionally intercut with the DOROTHY evocation. It's a conversation that GREGORY is having with ANDY, the boy he has replaced in goal. During this match ANDY hangs around the goal mouth. He has turned up out of dedication and curiosity, and also to give GREGORY bits of advice when the ball gets too close for comfort.

ANDY   This is a real farce. Nine games lost in a row and what do we do? Sack the goalie and put a girl in the forward line. It's a madhouse.

GREGORY   Watch the game Andy, watch the game. She's good, she can move.

ANDY   It's not right, it's unnatural. It doesn't even *look* nice.

GREGORY   It's modern, Andy, it's good. Modern girls, modern boys. It's tremendous – look.

DOROTHY   Get back.

ANDY   Girls weren't meant to play football, it's too tough, too physical.

GREGORY Tough? Have you ever watched them playing hockey? They're like wild animals. Even at twelve and thirteen, they'd kill you. You know, hockey was invented by Red Indians as a form of torture. They used to make the cowboys play the squaws.

ANDY Shite! That was lacrosse. And anyway if women were meant to play football they'd have their tits somewhere else. They weren't designed for football. Gregory!

The play has made its way towards GREGORY's goal. They're both in a mild panic.

ANDY Watch the ball, go out and meet it, don't wait for it. Watch the winger, he's coming up fast, wait for the cross.

Suddenly the play is upon them. ANDY stands back, powerless to do any more. In an instant GREGORY is surrounded by fast-moving bodies. Hanging on to ANDY's few words of advice, he's come forward to 'meet the ball', but he makes too much of an effort and the play is already past him and his goal is open. ANDY, helpless, mimes a perfect save from behind the goal, his movements coming from instinct and frustration. GREGORY collects the ball from the back of the net. DOROTHY snaps her fingers at him and demands the ball. She's eager to get the game under way again. She doesn't have time even to be indifferent to GREGORY right now.

DOROTHY Greg, come on, give us the ball.

DOROTHY takes the ball upfield. Two BOYS are watching GREGORY.

IST BOY What a prick!

GREGORY I took my eye off the ball for a split second, two micro-seconds.

ANDY   We need more women in this team, more
        new blood.

GREGORY   Yes, she's some girl.

DOROTHY scores a goal.

ANDY   What a goal. What a girl. Yes, she's got a nice
        pair of legs as well.

GREGORY   Andy, please. (*The PLAYERS cluster round
           DOROTHY.*) Look at that! It's disgusting.
           That's – that's perverse. In a football field,
           with kids watching. Come on, there's a game
           to be played! That's the sort of thing that
           gives football a bad name! That is disgusting.
           Oh!

IST BOY   That's a girl.

2ND BOY   You're a genius, Robert. You're a genius.

19   Int. Dressing Room. Day.   19

GREGORY is alone now. Maybe he's had to hang around for a
while to avoid ending up in the showers with that boy. He's
wearing only his shorts and is drying his hair at a mirror
with a nifty electric hair dryer. DOROTHY, of all people,
comes in. She has just come from a shower and has slipped
back into her football shirt and pants. She is paying a lot of
attention to a small cut on her leg, and not too much attention
goes on GREGORY, at first anyway.

DOROTHY   D'you have any plasters in here? There's
           none next door.

GREGORY is taken aback by her sudden arrival. He puts
down the hair dryer and out of modesty or silliness he covers
his nipples with the middle finger of each hand. Then, more
sensibly, he reaches for a sweatshirt and pulls it on.

GREGORY   No. Maybe. I'll get some.

He's eager to be helpful. DOROTHY hardly notices. She is sitting down, completely absorbed in examining her wound, although she has a detached, objective attitude to it. GREGORY is doing enough whining for both of them anyway.

DOROTHY   Don't panic, it's just a scratch. I only want to save my tights getting blood on them. That big gorilla on the left wing – I got my own back. I got my boot on his shin and scraped it right down. Big animal.

GREGORY's face reacts a little delicately to this. He tries to latch onto the mood of things, however.

GREGORY   You'll have a bruise there.

DOROTHY   Not if I let it bleed. That's the idea. I don't bruise easily.

You bet your sweet life she doesn't.

GREGORY   I do. I bruise like a peach. (*He hits himself on the chest to make the point.*) Bruise.

DOROTHY has only paid fleeting attention to this. She is still self-absorbed, although her attention has wandered to a tiny scar on her other knee. She points it out to GREGORY, taking his interest for granted.

DOROTHY   See that? I was only three when that happened. I was chasing a wee boy on the beach. I wasn't going to hurt him. I fell on a bottle. That'll never go away. I'm marked for life. I'm imperfect.

The bit about being imperfect is her little joke. They laugh.

GREGORY   No, no. It's nice. I like it.

DOROTHY   Really?

Another concession she allows admirers is the illusion that they can have original opinions about her.

GREGORY is getting carried away with this intimacy all of a sudden granted him.

> GREGORY I hurt my arm once, at the joint. I can't get it any higher than this. (*He raises his left arm to head level.*) I used to be able to get it away up here.

He raises the same arm right above his head.

> DOROTHY You just did.

> GREGORY No, it's this arm. It's stuck.

He now goes through the pantomime with his other arm, stuck at head level, stretching out of his seat to get it higher. They both laugh.

Their intimacy has reached a nice relaxed stage now. DOROTHY has one more treat for him. She indicates another scar at the back of her neck, a little bit down her back.

> DOROTHY Look at this, then – my big brother threw a bike at me. I was only seven. I can only see it in the mirror. It's quite nice isn't it? Nice shape.

> GREGORY Yeah. (*Clears throat*) Yeah.

> DOROTHY Renaldo, that was a boy in Italy last summer, he said it was like a new moon, very romantic, 'la luna'.

> GREGORY Ah, si, si, bella, bella!

He's up against the ropes, but he's still fighting.

> DOROTHY Ah, parliamo italiano!

> GREGORY No, not really, just bella, bella.

> DOROTHY Oh. I think it's a wonderful language. So

35

	alive. I want to live in Italy when I leave school.
GREGORY	Oh.
DOROTHY	I can speaka de language. I'm a quarter Italian and a quarter Irish, on my mother's side.

GREGORY brightens up again.

| GREGORY | Hey, I can speak Irish. |

A little giggle between them.

GREGORY	What was Renaldo doing down there anyway?
DOROTHY	He lives there.
GREGORY	(*indicating her back*) I mean down there.
DOROTHY	Ah, he was putting some suntan oil on for me.
GREGORY	Bella, bella.

They fall into a short silence.

| GREGORY | Anything else to show me? |

DOROTHY looks at him blankly.

| GREGORY | Any major wounds when you were twelve? Fourteen? |

DOROTHY catches on and they both smile. Another quite happy silence between them, mainly because GREGORY is wondering where he goes from here. Just then the door is thrown open, the spell is broken, and in come GORDON and ERIC. GORDON is the sixteen-year-old ace reporter from the school magazine. ERIC is his side-kick the photographer (he's the same guy who didn't have his camera with him that night at the Nurses' Hostel). They have come to interview DOROTHY.

GORDON   Oh, hi, Dorothy. Nice to see you. Good game? Look I'd like to have a chat with you for the school magazine. I want to interview you, and that girl in 2A that had the triplets. You're pretty famous now, you know.

GREGORY tries desperately to retrieve their intimacy.

GREGORY   I'm sorry, this is a dressing room. You can't come in here.

This gambit of GREGORY's is completely ignored.

GORDON is pretty much in command now.

GORDON   Eric, get the whole dressing room thing, and some nice big close shots of Dorothy. You don't mind if Eric flashes do you?

GREGORY has a last effort. He takes ERIC aside and tries to appeal to him on all the wrong grounds, i.e. morally and as a friend.

GREGORY   This is no place for a camera, Eric. People take their clothes off in here.

ERIC   (*in a whisper to GREGORY*) Yeah – where better? (*more publicly to GREGORY*) Look, could you stand in here – too many shadows. Just keep well in there, will you? Thanks.

GREGORY, defeated, sits in his allotted place.

GORDON   I like to interview people like this – no preparation, everything nice and natural. Now tell me Dorothy, how are the boys taking it, you being in the team now?

GREGORY sees another chance, although he's clutching at straws.

GREGORY   You guys are so predictable, always trying to make trouble. We're all very happy. Dorothy is a very good player.

GORDON (*as meek as a lamb, hurt even*) Slow down
Gregory. This is an in-depth interview.
Dorothy?

DOROTHY Things are fine. I'm quicker than most boys,
so I can keep out of trouble. I take dancing
lessons too, and that helps my balance. What
you've got to realise is that my body's
quite . . . different.

GORDON Mmm. You've got a good body. You must
train a lot, keep in shape. Do you have time
for anything else? What do you and your
body do on Saturday night for instance?

DOROTHY Saturday nights are special. I like to do
something special.

GREGORY has caught GORDON's drift and is paying the
utmost attention to his technique, because he's appalled by it
and also because he wants to know how to do it. He's
fascinated.

GORDON How about doing something special this
Saturday?

GREGORY has had enough. Let's hope he's also learned
enough.

GREGORY Come on! This is a dressing room. You lot go
and conduct your business somewhere else.

He only meant GORDON and ERIC but,

DOROTHY I'll go and change too.

GORDON OK Dorothy. You're an interesting girl you
know. But I want to find the real Dorothy –
the one underneath the football strip.
Dorothy the woman. OK? Cheerio Gregory.

GREGORY Arrivederci Gordon. Hurry back.

The three of them leave. GREGORY resumes his hair drying. We can tell he's upset because he's muttering to himself, and being too violent with the hair dryer.

GREGORY   Bella, bella, bella, bella, bella, Renaldo, bella
           Gordon.

He looks into the mirror and does a parody of DOROTHY, in an imitation of her voice.

GREGORY   I like to do something special on Saturday
           night. Bella, bella.

20 Int. Classroom. Day.   20

GREGORY has accosted the Italian teacher, MISS FORD.

MISS FORD What's the sudden need to speak Italian,
           Gregory?

GREGORY   It's not sudden. I've been thinking about it
           for three years. It's taken a while to make up
           my mind.

MISS FORD is seated at her desk. GREGORY is leaning down close to her, his elbows on her desk. He's very tall so is almost bent double.

MISS FORD It's very late in the term to start.

GREGORY   I've got some free time. I'll catch up. It's very
           important to me as I want to live in Italy
           when I leave school.

MISS FORD You've been there, have you?

GREGORY   No. I've been to Ireland though. And I met
           some Italians there. They told me all about it.
           In English. Renaldo could speak good
           English.

MISS FORD Renaldo? Is that your Italian friend?

GREGORY   Not just him. There were girls there too. I just
           said Renaldo because he could speak good
           English.

MISS FORD Well, what kind of work do you want to do in
           Italy?

GREGORY   Well, I'd just learn the language and then I'll
           see what there is going.

MISS FORD You know, you should think about taking a
           course in Technical Italian.

GREGORY   Is that words to do with work and engines?

MISS FORD Uh-huh.

The whole thing sounds a bit grubby to GREGORY. He has an
image of working in a filling station, filling up Renaldo's
Maserati with petrol so that DOROTHY and Renaldo can
zoom down the autostrada to the beach, leaving GREGORY to
talk to the petrol-pump girls in Technical Italian.

GREGORY   I think I'd rather do the normal Italian, and
           work my way down.

MISS FORD Well, we'll leave it just now. I'll have a word
           with your form teacher. See what he can
           come up with. OK? I'm really pleased that
           you're interested. It's a lovely country.

GREGORY   Oh yeah, wonderful language. Don't you
           think it's so alive?

MISS FORD Did you manage to pick any of it up at all?

GREGORY   A couple of words.

MISS FORD waits expectantly.

GREGORY   Bella . . . and bella. Are there any words you
           could teach me just now?

MISS FORD Ti diró. Ti diró.

GREGORY Ti diró.

MISS FORD laughs.

MISS FORD It means I'll let you know, Gregory. OK?

GREGORY Yes. Ti diró. Ti diró.

21   Int. Chemistry Classroom. Day.   21

SUSAN and DOROTHY are working on an experiment.

DOROTHY What about Alan? D'you think he's still a virgin?

SUSAN No. He's been in the school orchestra for over a year now.

DOROTHY Pass the sulphuric acid, will you?

SUSAN hands her the bottle.

SUSAN What's the pH in that?

DOROTHY Seven.

SUSAN How's the football going?

DOROTHY Oh, it's good. You need to cut that up a bit. It's too thick.

SUSAN What about the goalie, Gregory?

DOROTHY Hm?

SUSAN What d'you make of Gregory?

DOROTHY Oh, he's a bit slow.

SUSAN And a bit awkward.

DOROTHY Yeah – slow and awkward.

SUSAN He's got a nice laugh.

DOROTHY Give me the bromide.

22   Int. School Corridor. Day.   22

BOY dressed as a Penguin comes down the corridor as ALEC comes up.

>ALEC Hey – Room 4.

The BOY dressed as a Penguin comes back and out through the doors. ALEC goes back into the room.

23   Int. Classroom. Day.   23

ANDY, CHARLIE and SUSAN.

>ANDY Good afternoon.

SUSAN doesn't look up.

>ANDY Do you know that when you sneeze it comes
>out your nose at one hundred miles an hour?

SUSAN looks up at ANDY and then down again.

>ANDY It's a well-known fact – one hundred miles an
>hour. Pwfff! Just like that.

SUSAN collects her books and stands up. She leaves.

24   Int. School Corridor. Day.   24

The BOY dressed as Penguin again, walking past TEACHER.

>TEACHER Room 16? Hurry up.

In a similar corridor PHIL walks through, and then GREGORY walks by, repeating his Italian phrase.

25   Int. Classroom. Day.   25

This is what GREGORY is late for. All his friends are here: STEVE, ANDY, ERIC and some of the girls, including

DOROTHY and her friends. The teacher is a young and very attractive thing called MISS WELCH.

GREGORY comes into the room. ANDY reads from
A Midsummer Night's Dream in a dull monotone. As the scene progresses, fewer and fewer PUPILS pay attention.

> ANDY   Here comes my messenger. How now, mad
>   spirit?
> What night-rule now about this haunted
>   grove?
> My mistress with a monster is in love.
> Near to her close and consecrated bower,
> While she was in her dull and sleeping hour,
> A crew of patches, rude mechanicals,
> That work for bread upon Athenian stalls,
> Were met together to rehearse a play
> Intended for great Theseus' nuptial day.
> The shallowest thick-skin of that barren sort,
> Who Pyramus presented, in their sport
> Forsook his scene and entered in a brake,
> When I did him at this advantage take,
> And forth my mimic comes. When they him
>   spy –
> As wild geese that the creeping fowler eye,
> Sever themselves, and madly sweep the sky –
> So at his sight away his fellows fly.

A shuffle of seats and rustle of books. GREGORY is sitting across the aisle from STEVE, slightly behind him. The class settles down. A few squeaks alert us at first. Seen behind a couple of reading PUPILS, we see two hands applying water to the windows, on the outside. Some more squeaks and two faces slide up into view on the far side of the glass. Some more squeaks and the windowcleaners are in full view, suspended in their gondola three storeys above the playground. They work away, giving the impression of being slightly apologetic at intruding on the quiet classroom scene. They don't want to make a fuss.

The windowcleaners are MR HALL and BILLY, his young apprentice. BILLY was until very recently on the other side of the glass, a pupil in this very school, in fact a classmate of GREGORY's. MR HALL has caught sight of DOROTHY. He says something to BILLY and discreetly points her out. BILLY nods and smiles and says a few words back to him. Some of the pupils have taken notice of the windowcleaners by now. MR HALL has even caught DOROTHY's eye. He performs a little pantomime for her: he wraps up a lighted cigarette in his polishing cloth, gives it the magic once-over, and hey presto, opens it out and the cigarette has gone. Then he finds it behind his ear. DOROTHY smiles. GREGORY has seen them and smiles too. Then BILLY catches STEVE's eye (they were good pals). They wave enthusiastically.

> STEVE Please Miss, there's Billy out there.

MISS WELCH looks up. She liked BILLY and is genuinely pleased to see him. She goes over to the window and shouts out to him. The big windows don't open.

> ANDY Here o'er and o'er one falls.
> He 'Murder!' cries, and help from Athens
>   calls.
> Their sense thus weak, lost with their fears
>   thus strong,

> MISS WELCH Be quiet, Andy.

> ANDY Made senseless things begin to do them
>   wrong.
> For briars and thorns at their apparel snatch,

> MISS WELCH Hello Billy! Nice of you to drop in.

> ANDY Some sleeves, some hats; from yielders all
>   things catch.
> I led them on . . .

A GIRL finally gets him to stop.

MISS WELCH Well, you said you would come back and see me again!

BILLY Here I am.

MR HALL is shuffling around in the background, if there is a background in a windowcleaner's gondola. BILLY has learned a few adult social niceties.

BILLY Can I introduce my boss? Miss Welch, this is Mr Hall. It's his own business.

MR HALL is determined to observe the social niceties to the limit. He contorts himself to get his hand through the gap in the window. Miss Welch takes what has the appearance of a disembodied hand and shakes it.

MISS WELCH Pleased to meet you. Well, how's our Billy shaping up?

MR HALL He's a good lad. He's been telling me about all the characters in the school. He likes you. And he's washed a few windows as well.

MISS WELCH I hope you're doing mine for free Billy – well, for old times' sake?

BILLY Give me your glasses and I'll do them as well. No charge.

She fetches out her spectacles to him, and he gives them a professional rub with a clean chamois.

MISS WELCH Thank you.

BILLY See you outside at four, lads, eh?

MISS WELCH Listen, why don't you come up and see me sometime?

BILLY I'll do that. I'll use the stairs though.

ANDY I led them on in this distracted fear,
And left sweet Pyramus translated there;
When in that moment– so it came to pass –

Titania waked, and straightway loved an ass.

MR HALL and BILLY get back to work, and so does the class. BILLY catches STEVE's eye again and mimes to him, 'See you at four o'clock outside, after school?' STEVE gets the message and nods 'affirmative'. GREGORY has been a happy onlooker of the whole scene. He nods enthusiastically too, more or less to himself, and presumes his involvement in the rendezvous at four.

26   Int. Head's Office, Day.   26

HEAD'S OFFICE. OUTER ROOM. PHIL is waiting to be seen by the HEAD. He sits uneasily watching the office door.

Inside the HEAD is in conversation with STEVE. They sit at opposite sides of his big desk. The HEAD is in a casual pose, and STEVE seems at his ease as well.

> HEAD   Doughnuts.

> STEVE   Well, we're still doing two kinds. There's jam-filled and rings.

> HEAD   What kind of jam?

> STEVE   What would you like?

> HEAD   Blackcurrant?

> STEVE   That's no problem.

The HEAD leans back in his chair for a moment or two's thought.

> HEAD   I'll have half a dozen – OK?

STEVE makes a note on his writing-pad. The wheeling and dealing proceeds at a very casual pace.

> STEVE   Half a dozen. I tell you what – I'll throw in a couple of ring doughnuts. There are usually some left on a Friday anyway.

> HEAD Good.

> STEVE Have you given the petits choux any more
> thought?

> HEAD What was that again?

> STEVE It was a basic choux pastry. I've been
> working on it. I think I've got it perfect.

HEAD tastes some pastry.

> HEAD That's good, that's very good.

27   Int. Head's Outer Room. Day.   27

PHIL is *still* waiting. The door to the HEAD's office opens and
the HEAD shows STEVE out of the room. As they exit, PHIL
stands up and STEVE has to squeeze past him.

> HEAD I'd like everything in my office by three
> o'clock on Friday. Is that understood?

> STEVE Yes sir.

PHIL seems pleased with what he presumably thinks is a
stern command on the part of the HEAD. He almost gives
STEVE a kind of 'so there!' gesture.

When STEVE exits, PHIL goes into the HEAD's office.

> PHIL I'm sorry, I'm early . . .

> HEAD Have a seat, Mr Menzies.

The HEAD closes the outer door.

28   Int. Head's Office. Day.   28

The HEAD crosses from the door and sits behind his desk.
PHIL sits alertly, waiting for the HEAD to begin.

The HEAD takes his time, collecting his thoughts, then,

> HEAD There's a girl in the football team.

This bald statement doesn't give PHIL too much to go on in terms of the HEAD's feelings about the matter. Tricky ground for PHIL. He would have preferred an outright reaction that he could fall into line with.

> PHIL Well . . . yes and no.

> HEAD Yes and no.

> PHIL Yes.

The HEAD isn't helping PHIL in the least.

> HEAD What d'you mean?

> PHIL Well, we *could* have a girl in the football team if we wanted one.

> HEAD Do we want one?

> PHIL Well . . .

The HEAD decides to let PHIL off the hook.

> HEAD I think it's a wonderful idea, terrific.

> PHIL Yes! And she's a great wee player. She won't hold the team back one little bit!

The HEAD halts him before he gets too carried away.

> HEAD One possible problem area. The showers. What happens about the showers?

> PHIL Oh, she'll bring her own soap.

> HEAD And you'll undertake to keep everything above board?

> PHIL Oh, oh yes. I'll most definitely, most definitely.

RICHARD leans against a pole, whistling. CHILDREN pass by on either side. MADELINE comes forward with other CHILDREN.

RICHARD Hello.

MADELINE Hello.

RICHARD Carry your bag for you?

MADELINE I can't see you today. I've got to go up to the big school.

RICHARD What for?

MADELINE Oh, family trouble.

RICHARD Is it Gregory?

MADELINE Guess what – he's fallen in love!

RICHARD That's big trouble. Well, maybe I can see you later on.

MADELINE Right. Bye bye.

RICHARD Bye.

30   Ext. School. Day.   30

MADELINE's outside Gregory's school. We see her take up her position outside the 'Big School', as patient and as self-contained as anything. GREGORY spots her from an upstairs window. We see his point of view of the tiny figure resting on a bollard at the main gate. She looks up – there must be telepathy between them – and they exchange a wave and a smile. MADELINE and GREGORY are very, very close; they love each other in fact, and make a very touching couple. They work too well together to be labelled 'the odd couple', so let's put that out of our heads.

GREGORY gets back to his work and MADELINE gets back to her waiting.

A car draws up at the school gate. It's MR HALL's car, maybe a Datsun, or a mature Rover, with a roof-rack and some ladders on the rack (in these days of gondolas the ladders are more of a trademark than an appliance). BILLY exits from the car, now dressed very neatly in a sports jacket, crisp shirt with open collar, and tailored pants. The young man's ideal of casual elegance. MR HALL drives off and BILLY and MADELINE wait on. It's just a matter of time until one of them says something to the other.

> BILLY Cigarette? Waiting for somebody?

MADELINE Yes.

> BILLY You're not giving much away. There are two thousand people in there.

MADELINE Gregory, fourth year.

> BILLY Oh, Steve's pal. Are you Gregory's girl?

MADELINE I'm Madeline.

A last shot of them waiting.

31   Ext. School. Day.   31

At four o'clock, STEVE and GREGORY and ANDY and CHARLIE come out of school and make their way to the main gate. By now BILLY and MADELINE are well into a relaxed conversation. They are sitting on the wall together and MADELINE is laughing at something BILLY has told her. She is still very much the lady though. No matter how funny the joke was she can still make out she is laughing from politeness.

The BOYS approach MADELINE and BILLY.

> BILLY She's fancied me since first years. She's after

> my body. I might have to give in. (*Then he mimics her.*) 'Why don't you come up and see me some time.'

STEVE rushes towards BILLY as if in a frenzy of desire.

BILLY Hey, watch the jacket! I had to wet, wash and polish eighty-four windows for this!

GREGORY That's some job. D'you get danger money for that?

BILLY No, but if I die, my mother gets her windows washed for nothing for twenty-five years. Inside and out. (*He gets a little more serious.*) I'll tell you what you need danger money for . . . it's the women. There's something about windowcleaners that just turns them on, specially up in the Logan Vale Estate – you know the private houses. They spend too much time on their own up there. So *we* turn up once a week. Singing songs, telling jokes.

CHARLIE Washing the windows.

BILLY Right. Washing the windows. Then, before you know it, round to the back door, 'Hello darling, can you give us some hot water?'

ANDY I don't get it.

GREGORY Hot water, is that a code?

BILLY No. It's for washing the windows. But that's just to get the conversation going. *Anything* can happen after that.

STEVE I suppose the worst thing that could happen is that they give you some hot water.

BILLY Yeah, that sometimes happens.

By now they are walking up the road, the five BOYS in a group with MADELINE following a few paces behind them. She's letting them get on with their silly conversation, as always dominated by talk of sex. She has a very worldly attitude to it, although GREGORY gives her frequent anxious glances when the conversation gets, to his mind, spicey.

CHARLIE We saw something great last week, you know, a nurse up at the hostel. Tits, bum, fanny, the lot!

BILLY Oh, I can see that fifty times a day through a window. It's *contact*, the thing, doing it.

ANDY Have you done it?

BILLY Eleven times.

STEVE In one night?

BILLY No. Different times. There's something new always crops up.

ANDY What d'you mean? Stuff like foreplay?

BILLY Foreplay's important. As long as you know, it's leading up to something. Otherwise it's just fooling around.

MADELINE and GREGORY take a different road here.

GREGORY I'll see you guys later, right? See you, Billy.

BILLY Bye bye Madeline. If I don't see you through the week, I'll see you through the window.

MADELINE and GREGORY go off down the road.

BILLY They grow up fast don't they?

CHARLIE Ten years old, with a body of a woman of thirteen.

32   Ext. Children's Playground. Day.

Don't get MADELINE wrong. Supersmart little girls have been done to death on the screen lately. MADELINE is not a Jody O'Neal or a Tatum Foster. We want her to come over not as a child/adult monster, but as a *woman*.

One more thought *vis-à-vis* MADELINE and GREGORY, from Christine De Rivoyre: ' . . . there are all manner of betrothals here on earth, and all are blessed if the heart be true . . .'.

MADELINE You need some new trousers. These baggy ones are awful. I'll talk to mum about it. Blue ones, Italian. If you're going to start falling in love, you'll have to start taking care of yourself.

GREGORY Are Italians good dressers?

MADELINE Yeah, they make nice trousers. They've got style. I was talking to Steve's sister about Dorothy. She's very attractive. I *knew* you would fall for that type.

GREGORY She's quarter Italian.

MADELINE Don't get too serious about her, if you can help it. Have you asked her out yet? (*GREGORY shakes his head.*) I can help you. I can tell you things. I'm a girl. You were nice to me when other boys *hated* their sisters.

33   Ext. Shopping Plaza. Day.   33

Outside a shop window. The conversation takes place in isolated bursts, MADELINE doing most of the talking, in between darting in and out of shops and pointing things out to GREGORY in shop windows. There are pauses in the dialogue while GREGORY hangs around outside a shop while she is inside involved in some deal or other.

GREGORY   If it was brown it would be OK. Not enough
           brown in it. Yeah. There's a dark brown.
           Well, the grey was quite nice too.

MADELINE   You don't *think* about colours, do you? If you
           don't take an interest in yourself, how can
           you expect other people to be interested in
           you? Talk to Dorothy. Ask her out. She won't
           say no, I'll bet you. But don't treat her too
           special. You're too romantic, it could scare a
           girl off.

GREGORY   What kind of things should I say?

MADELINE   For goodness sake, don't plan it. Don't think
           about it, *do* it!

34   Int. Café. Day.   34

We find GREGORY and MADELINE inside a café.

GREGORY   So I should think less about love and more
           about colours.

MADELINE   You've got it.

The waitress comes up for their order.

WAITRESS   What would you like?

MADELINE   A ginger-beer and lime juice with ice cream
           please, but don't stir it.

GREGORY   Coffee please.

WAITRESS   Black or white?

He looks at MADELINE. He knows he's going to blow it.

GREGORY   Brown.

MADELINE releases a sigh, but she's only acting up for fun.

GREGORY   Don't do *blue* coffees here, Madeline. This
          isn't Italy. No style.

MADELINE (*getting a bit serious*) Do you dream about
          her? (*GREGORY nods.*) That means you love
          her. It's the one you have the dreams about
          that counts.

A pause.

GREGORY   What do you dream about?

MADELINE Just ginger-beer and ice cream. I'm still a
          little girl, remember?

By now the drinks have arrived.

GREGORY   That looks nice. Is it?

MADELINE Is it? (*Toying with her drink*)The nicest part is
          just before you taste it. Your mouth goes all
          tingly. But that can't go on forever.

She drinks.

35   Int. Gregory's House. Day.   35

STEVE has come to call. They are in GREGORY's sitting room
watching the TV. At least STEVE is watching it. The
programme is a cookery demonstration, and STEVE reacts to
it much as a more straightforward guy would react to a
football match on telly, engrossed and critical. GREGORY is
uninterested. He would rather be talking about DOROTHY.
STEVE shouts the odd remark at the TV while GREGORY
makes attempts to engage him in conversation. We hear
snatches of the sound from the TV. Apart from them the
house is empty.

GREGORY   D'you know anything about Italians?

STEVE responds a bit this time but still doesn't take his eyes
from the screen.

STEVE   Excellent seafood in the north-west. Some of
their regional pasta dishes are good too.
Good with salads, very stylish all round.
Whoa, whoa! Go easy with the sugar, lady.

GREGORY, heavens above, gets angry.

GREGORY   Food! Food! Food! Is that all you think
about? You're *unnatural* pal, you're a freak!

STEVE is more bewildered than hurt at the outburst.
GREGORY eats.

STEVE   You eat it, don't you? I've never seen you
turn up your nose at anything I've made.

He's acting more hurt now that it occurs to him.

STEVE   Hours and hours I've spent, making you
lovely, lovely things. And all it means to you
in the end is *food*.

GREGORY   Look pal, I don't know whether you've
noticed, but I'm going through a *crisis*.

STEVE   Of course I've noticed, but what do you want
me to do? The whole world's got problems.
You're just *obsessed* by a beautiful, young,
unattainable girl – so what?

GREGORY   Stop saying things like 'obsessed' and
'unattainable' – it's love.

STEVE   OK, it's love. Go and attain her then. Sweep
her off her feet. Oh, I forgot, you're the
goalkeeper, *she's* the sweeper.

GREGORY   Ha, ha.

STEVE   Look, one key question. Have you talked to
her, asked her for a date? Anything?

GREGORY shakes his head.

STEVE   Well do it. *Then* complain.

GREGORY thinks for a second or two.

GREGORY If I get a date, can I borrow your white jacket?

STEVE (*emphatically*) No.

By this time GREGORY has made his way over to STEVE's chair, and is kneeling beside him, their heads are close together and they face each other in a challenging but still friendly way. The doorbell rings. Both of them react to it.

STEVE Maybe that's her.

GREGORY makes for the door.

36   Ext. Gregory's Front Door. Evening.   36

GREGORY looks to right and left when he opens the door. He's slightly baffled because nobody appears to be there. Then he looks *down*. He finds RICHARD, who is ten years old and as confident and daunting as MADELINE. Added to this the fact that GREGORY *hates* male children.

RICHARD I wonder if Maddy's in?

GREGORY You mean Madeline. She's out with her mother.

RICHARD That's a shame. I thought we could go for a walk. Maybe I could wait.

GREGORY No. They'll be ages.

RICHARD Maybe she could phone me later on. She has my number.

GREGORY Who are you anyway? You're talking about my sister and she doesn't go for walks with *anybody*. What's the idea, coming to people's doors, seducing people's sisters? Act your age, go and break some windows, demolish some phone boxes. When I was your age . . .

RICHARD (*interrupts*) You're Gregory aren't you? (*He offers GREGORY his hand. GREGORY gives his without thinking, and his outraged speech tails off.*) How are you feeling? Everything OK?

GREGORY retrieves his hand and gets his outrage under way again. He laughs.

GREGORY There's nothing wrong with me, son. You're the one that should be worried. Seducing children. You're a freak. You're heading for big trouble – under-age walks – dates. You'll run out of vices before you're twelve if you don't slow down. Hoi – piss off.

RICHARD figures he's got a nut on his hands.

RICHARD OK Gregory, fair enough. Ask Maddy to call me anyway.

He beats a rational man's retreat down the path. GREGORY feels in command now and shouts after him.

GREGORY The name's *Madeline*. Go on, piss off! Get.

37   Gregory's Bedroom. Night.   37

GREGORY is quiet and alone. The rest of the house is sleeping. His bedroom is still the bedroom of a boy, with football posters and trophies and toys scattered amongst the newer trappings of manhood, which are still thin on the ground at this stage in GREGORY's career. He is tapping his drumsticks together, then throws them down. He looks at a magazine, and throws that down.

38   Ext. Gregory's House. Night.   38

GREGORY opens a blind and raises the window. A cat miaows. GREGORY miaows.

39 Int. Susan's Bedroom. Night. 39

SUSAN is reading in bed. She hears GREGORY's miaow. She smiles.

40 Int. Tunnel. Day. 40

SCHOOL CHILDREN move through the tunnel.

ANDY and CHARLIE walk through.

> ANDY I had that dream last night – that's four
> nights in a row. That's really good, that!

41 Int. Gregory's Bedroom. Day. 41

GREGORY sits at his drum kit.

42 Int. School Corridor. Day. 42

GREGORY has arrived and is making his way along the corridor. His walk seems more purposeful than his usual. He stops at a door marked 'DARKROOM' and knocks on it gently. From inside we hear a voice singing. It breaks off to shout to GREGORY. The voice belongs to ERIC.

> ERIC Yeah. Hold on, I'm in the dark!

After a few more moments of singing and bumping and banging, the door is opened. ERIC sticks his head out.

> ERIC What is it?

> GREGORY Can I come in?

ERIC ushers him in and as the door closes we find them in the eerie reddish diffused light of the darkroom.

> GREGORY You know, I'd make a lousy photographer.
> I get scared in the dark.

ERIC is already engrossed in his work, and doesn't get the joke, if GREGORY thought it was one.

> ERIC What d'you want?

> GREGORY I just wondered how the snaps came out, you know, the ones in the dressing room.

ERIC brightens up, and even ignores the reference to 'snaps'.

> ERIC Oh, Dorothy! I'm working on her now.

He gestures towards his trays of chemicals. They both huddle over the table and ERIC gets on with his printing.

> ERIC She's a beauty. She's a dream to photograph.

GREGORY plays it cool, as cool as he can.

> GREGORY Very interesting.

> ERIC I could go for this girl in a big way. Look at that nose!

We see an image of DOROTHY appear as the picture emerges in the developing tray. GREGORY is still playing Mr Cool.

> GREGORY Very pretty.

> ERIC Some of the guys reckon she's too much like a boy. I don't. I think she's wonderful.

> GREGORY Her like a boy? No. She's just modern.

ERIC is really enthusiastic now.

> ERIC You're right! It's modern! It's the future! In another million years there'll be no men, no women . . . just *people*. It's logical evolution. Evolution is the thing!

GREGORY is falling behind ERIC's advanced thinking.

> GREGORY No more men or women?

> ERIC (*triumphantly*) Just a whole world full of wankers. Drink?

GREGORY shakes his head. Then they get back to the printing business.

> ERIC Ah, this is a modern girl! Made to be photographed! Boy, I'd love to get my wide-angle lens on her. A low-key light, a soft fill.

To get his point across he goes through an elaborate mime, his arms waving about as he directs his imaginary lights here and there. He uses GREGORY's face as the imaginary DOROTHY. GREGORY remains still as ERIC gets really carried away.

> ERIC On her face and the body of the eighties I could really *make* that girl.
>
> (*He calms down, leaves GREGORY alone, and gets back to the printing machine.*) One elephant, two elephant, three elephant, four elephant, five elephant . . . (*GREGORY is curious.*) . . . six elephant. If you don't put the elephants in you don't get real seconds: ten elephants. (*He removes the print paper from the printer as the printing light goes off.*) Every print needs an exact exposure. This one needed ten elephants.

GREGORY nods knowingly, and huddles over the tray again.

> GREGORY Here she comes.

> ERIC (*to the photograph*) Yeah, you'll be a beauty. (*More to GREGORY*) Look how quickly Gordon moved in. He knows what he likes. I timed it, you know, one elephant, two elephant. One minute and fifty elephants and he had a date. That's a record, even for him!

GREGORY puts on a brave face.

> GREGORY Yeah, what a guy! What an absolutely really

incredible guy! What a guy! Absolutely!
(*GREGORY is making himself ill being
enthusaistic about GORDON. So he calms down
and gets down to business.*) Look, give us a
photograph will you?

ERIC gets interested.

> ERIC Oh I get it . . . you fancy her too, eh?

> GREGORY No, it's for a friend, somebody really shy.
> Just give us a photograph, eh?

> ERIC This is really expensive: chemicals and the
> paper. Really expensive.

> GREGORY Twenty pence.

> ERIC Forty.

> GREGORY Twenty-five.

> ERIC I'll frame it for a pound.

We see DOROTHY's image floating in the tray again.

> GREGORY I'll take it just the way it is, thanks.

ERIC reaches for a pile of photographs.

> ERIC Better give you a dry one, don't want you
> dripping all down the corridor.

The money changes hands. GREGORY leaves ERIC to his
litany of money-spinners, and sets off down the corridor.
Then something nice happens to him.

43 Int. School Corridor. Day. 43

A GIRL from one of the junior years catches up with
GREGORY. GREGORY is practising his Italian.

> GIRL Are you Gregory?

GREGORY turns around, and puts on an easeful, mature air.

62

Junior girls make him feel comfortable.

> GREGORY That's me sweetheart. Well, who wants to know?

> GIRL Dorothy wants to see you.

This rocks him. The mature act vanishes. He turns to jelly.

> GREGORY Dorothy?

> GIRL That's what I said. She'll be in Room 9 at breaktime, OK?

The girl leaves a shaken, perplexed GREGORY. He's too shocked to be elated yet.

44 Int. Boys' Toilet. Day.   44

A SMALL BOY by the basins is combing his hair in the mirror. GREGORY runs in, then turns to the BOY.

> GREGORY Give us your comb, eh?

> BOY No.

> GREGORY Give me your comb.

> BOY No.

GREGORY goes to him and they struggle.

GREGORY takes the comb, combs his hair, and gives it back.

> GREGORY Thanks pal.

45 Int. Room 9. Day.   45

GREGORY approaches, knocks lightly and sticks his head into the room. We cut inside. DOROTHY and four of her female friends are casually and slightly menacingly draped over chairs and desks. GREGORY had been expecting a more intimate get-together, but that has proved to be blind optimism. To her credit, on this occasion DOROTHY is the sweetest of the bunch, in this her very own lioness's den.

> GREGORY Hi Dorothy. I got your message.

> DOROTHY Good. I just wanted to know what you were up to at lunchtime.

Another spark of optimism lights up his face.

> GREGORY Oh, nothing that can't wait a million years.

> DOROTHY Will you help me out with some goal practice?

> GREGORY Yeah, sure.

> DOROTHY It'll speed things up. I want to practise goal shots at different angles.

> GREGORY I'll bring my compass. (*Just a smile from Dorothy.*) Good. Well, I'll see you at half-twelve then.

> DOROTHY Fine.

A real smile for him this time.

> GREGORY Good. See you.

A very happy GREGORY leaves Room 9. His visit has been a very minor event to the girls, and things go on as if nothing much has happened. CAROL continues to brush LIZ's long hair, not in a servile or doting way, it's just part of their mutual admiration/aid scheme. MARGO and HELEN and DOROTHY drift over to the windows and look down into the boys' playground, which at this time contains about nine hundred young males. The girls are seen against this background.

> MARGO Look at all these men.

> DOROTHY *Boys.*

> HELEN What's the difference?

They all have a little laugh. DOROTHY breaks into her favourite language. She uses it for important things.

> MARGO   Circa quindici centimetri a chacuno.

MARGO indicates sisse with her fingers. We close the scene on their faces.

46   Int. Boys' Toilets. Day.   46

GREGORY is hunting out STEVE, and he knows exactly where to find him. STEVE is a businessman, he's into retail bakery in a fairly serious way. All these hours slaving over a hot school oven aren't for nothing. He has two or three outlets for his buns and biscuits in the school. Breaktime is a busy time for STEVE, as he keeps an eye on sales and assesses future demands. So GREGORY figures that he'll find STEVE at his main place of business. That's why he heads for the boys' toilet.

In this scene STEVE is very businesslike, and is giving GREGORY only passing attention. GREGORY is the man with a mission, he wants STEVE's coat. It pays to have rich friends.

So GREGORY accosts him outside the toilet; an eager GREGORY confronting a STEVE involved in market trends bun-wise.

> GREGORY   (*breathless but cool, feeling good*) I'm on the way, Steve. It's off the ground – romance, it's in the air.
>
> STEVE   Hi pal!
>
> GREGORY   Can I have your jacket?
>
> STEVE   No.

They push their way into the toilet. It's a very different scene from GREGORY's solitary visit only minutes ago. The joint is jumping, the atmosphere is hazy, Cokes are being drunk, magazines are being swapped, tall stories are being eagerly told, a few old-fashioned people are having a quick drag on a cigarette. There's a hint of the speak-easy about the place. One or two people are combing their hair at the mirrors, but that's the only visible sign of the room's intended function. STEVE is one of the top men around here and makes his way through the clientele with ease, GREGORY at his heels.

GREGORY   I don't want to make a big thing of it. It's just that the jacket would really help. It would put the affair off on a proper footing. Just for one night, eh?

STEVE   What are you raving on about?

GREGORY   (*patiently*) Me. Dorothy. Date. It's in the bag. She's after me. She wants me to play with her at lunchtime.

STEVE deliberately gets the wrong idea.

STEVE   My, my, she wants you to play with her, eh? How do you do it Gregory?

GREGORY   *Football*, we're playing. I'm gonna be in goal.

STEVE   Not with my jacket, you won't.

By now they have reached the bakery counter, which is housed in one of the toilet cubicles. It is manned by one of STEVE's acolytes, KELVIN, a second-year fly-man. The cakes and biscuits are laid out on trays on top of the pristine porcelain.

STEVE   Morning Kelvin, how's business?

GREGORY   No! The jacket's for later, for the real date!

KELVIN   The doughnuts are going like hot cakes Steve, but the marzipan almonds don't seem to be everybody's cup of tea.

STEVE gives a sour glance around the clientele.

STEVE   (*almost to himself*) Tasteless sods!

GREGORY   Come on Steve, you gave Pete the jacket last
week. Why not me?

STEVE is now counting out the takings from KELVIN's little
money tin. He pockets most of it and drops back in a few
silver and a few copper coins.

STEVE   That's *exactly why*, Gregory old son. Did you
see that jacket the day after? Grass stains.
I don't know what kind of stains.

STEVE offers GREGORY a biscuit, a kind of 'we're still friends'
gesture. GREGORY nibbles a little delicately. He's very aware
of his surroundings.

GREGORY   Yeah, but with Dorothy and me things
would be high class. No stains, no.

STEVE sees a way to get off the hook.

STEVE   Look, I'll make a deal with you. You get the
date, signed, sealed, delivered, and then
come and ask me about the jacket – fair
enough?

KELVIN   Just keep the doughnuts coming Steve. We're
on the gravy train, but what the public says
is ease off on the marzipans.

STEVE and GREGORY are excited by now.

GREGORY   It's a deal. Would you like to throw in your
brown shoes as well?

STEVE affects a put-upon expression as they leave.

STEVE   I could use a persuasive prick like you in the
organisation. You could help me off-load
some marzipans onto an uncaring
population.

The scene closes with a general shot of the rabble in the
toilet, STEVE's uncaring public. Then GREGORY sees the
photographs of *Dorothy* on sale.

GREGORY I bought one of these this morning, and they cost me twenty-five pence.

BOY It's not my fault – see the boss.

47 Int. School Corridor. Day.

GREGORY walks forwards down the corridor.

Near the Darkroom can be heard:

ERIC (*out of view*) Thirty-one elephant, thirty-two elephant, thirty-three elephant.

GIRL laughs (*out of view*).

ERIC and GIRL (*out of view*) Thirty-four elephant, thirty-five elephant, thirty-six elephant.

48 Int. Kitchen. Day.

GIRL and DOROTHY talk together inaudibly.

49 Int. Dining Room. Day.

CHILDREN are getting served at the counter.

KELVIN speaks to a BOY who is being served.

KELVIN Don't touch that ravioli – it's garbage.

He goes off. PHIL MENZIES comes on with a bowl of soup.

PHIL Ravioli please. Thank you. (*PHIL sits next to BRENDA, whistle in soup.*) Hello, Brenda.

BRENDA Hello.

PHIL Mind if I join you? (*She shakes her head. PHIL sits.*) How's the lunch?

BRENDA The usual.

PHIL   Hmm. The meat looks OK. (*He notices his whistle in the soup.*) Ah – have you got a tissue?

He holds his whistle up. BRENDA gets her handbag.

ANDY and CHARLIE have picked up their food and are loitering in the stand-up bar area.

ANDY is scanning the dining room, looking for a likely couple of girls to 'move in' on. CHARLIE is his usual silent and undemonstrative self, following ANDY without question or comment.

ANDY indicates a couple of girls sitting at a four-place table. The girls are CAROL and MARGO.

ANDY   Let's sweet-talk these two. (*ANDY picks up his tray and moves in, followed by CHARLIE. They approach the girls' table.*) Good afternoon ladies.

CAROL   Hello.

ANDY   D'you mind if we join you?

The girls give a shrug of acquiescence. ANDY gives CHARLIE an encouraging look as they sit down.

ANDY smiles around the table. No great response from the girls so far. They eat on in silence. ANDY looks across the table to CHARLIE, and mimes a kind of 'do something, say something' gesture to him. No response from CHARLIE. ANDY ploughs on alone.

ANDY   How's your roast beef?

CAROL answers in a dry way.

CAROL   It's veal.

ANDY   Veal! D'you know how they make veal? They get the little baby calves and they hang them upside down. They slit their throats and let the blood drip out. It's very interesting, isn't it?

CAROL puts down her knife and fork, but doesn't offer up any other kind of response except to get up and leave the table.

50   Ext. Football Field. Day.   50

With lunchtime well under way we cut outside to the playing fields. We first see GREGORY and DOROTHY as small figures in a wide shot of the football field. They are up at one end of the field near the goal, and seem out of scale with the bigness of the field. We cut closer to them. DOROTHY looks good in a well-fitting strip with a loose sweatshirt top – training gear. GREGORY was caught on the hop this morning and has had to borrow a pair of shorts, and they are just a shade on the big side. He is affecting goalkeeper's gloves and hat.

Throughout this scene DOROTHY is diffident, wrapped up in her training and her own skill. We very quickly get the message that GREGORY is here to retrieve the ball for her and not much more . She takes her football seriously, and as the scene develops she can't help giving the odd bit of advice or criticism to GREGORY. She is full of concentration like one of these really wound-up lady tennis players at Wimbledon.

We get the scene under way as she bangs the ball past GREGORY and into the net from somewhere near the penalty spot. GREGORY doesn't get near the ball, and has to poke around at the back of the net to retrieve it.

GREGORY   This is great! I can really use this practice.

GREGORY gives the ball back to DOROTHY.

DOROTHY   Thanks.

GREGORY   Good goal.

DOROTHY   Just kick it out in future. It'll be much quicker.

GREGORY Good idea. Great idea. I'll do that next time, eh?

DOROTHY moves from the ball, turns her back on the goal, gathers herself together and races for the ball. When she reaches it she turns on a sixpence in an instant and gets off another cracking shot. The ball seems to curve in mid-air and bend round into the far side of the goal out of GREGORY's reach. His efforts at stopping the ball are so unrelated to its movements that he seems to be playing in a different game, a phantom game all of his own.

GREGORY (*enthusiastic as ever*) Great shot! You got me that time!

The ball once more goes back to DOROTHY.

DOROTHY Could you stop dancing around so much, it's very distracting.

She lines up another shot from far out on the wing.

DOROTHY How can you judge a shot dancing around like . . .

The ball's in the net again.

GREGORY (*his vocabulary is getting limited*) Great! First class!

We are close in on DOROTHY's face this time as she lines up the shot. She's up to something. Maybe she wants to teach this noisy overgrown ball-boy a lesson.

GREGORY is still bouncing around in the goal.

GREGORY You're some girl. I haven't got near the ball yet.

Spoken just too soon. The ball is hammered into his stomach. In reflex motion his hands curve into his groin and capture the ball. The force of the shot seems to have moved him back into the goal, like a cowboy being shot off his feet in a movie. He falls.

DOROTHY (*allows herself a smile*) Well held. You OK?

GREGORY Huh.

DOROTHY Come on. We've only got another hour.

GREGORY is on his knees with an overdone smile on his face. This love racket is really hard work.

GREGORY I think I've broken my neck-chain.

GREGORY fumbles around in the dirt for a moment or two, searching for his precious chain. For DOROTHY the fun is over and she wants to get back to work. She is working expertly and energetically with the ball, foot-juggles, two-touch shoulder-juggles, neck-traps, flick-ups, while GREGORY gets himself together.

GREGORY is more or less ready, but an hour seems like a very long time to him all of a sudden.

DOROTHY (*really energised now*) Come on, come on.
Tackle me, try and block, then move back
and block some more. And use your feet.
Don't grab for the ball.

GREGORY OK, OK, keep them coming, Dorothy.

It looks like GREGORY is a long way away from asking for that date. Circumstances are working against him. It's not exactly candlelight and roses out there. Let's leave him to work on it for a bit.

51 Int. Staffroom. Day.   51

PHIL is cleaning his whistle. He looks at himself in the mirror. Then he blows his whistle. ALISTAIR starts.

52   Int. Music Room. Day.   52

The HEAD is playing the organ. PUPILS are going to lessons.
BOY watches HEAD who finally notices.

> HEAD   Off you go, you small boys.

HEAD resumes playing.

53   Int. Dining Room. Day.   53

ANDY and CHARLIE are very desolate-looking. They
continue to pick at their food.

> ANDY   Of course you know we're in the wrong
> place. (*They munch some more.*) You know
> where we should be? (*Another pause for
> eating*) South America. (*Not much reaction
> from CHARLIE*) There's a town there, and –
> this is a well-known fact – look, do you know
> what the ratio of women to men is there?
> (*CHARLIE doesn't signal a reply.*) Eight to one.
> It's eight women per one guy! That's the
> kind of place for us, eh? (*CHARLIE gives a nod
> this time.*) It's called *Caracas*.

We end the scene by cutting to a wider shot of ANDY and
CHARLIE alone at their table amongst the general hubbub.

54   Ext. Football Field. Day.   54

GREGORY and DOROTHY are leaving the field. GREGORY is
panting and sweating, mud on his face and legs and football
strip. He walks with the stagger of near exhaustion.
DOROTHY is cool and clean and serene.

> DOROTHY   Are you happy in goal?

> GREGORY   (*breathing heavily*) It's OK.

DOROTHY   You waste a lot of energy. No control.

GREGORY   (*bravely*) Got tons left.

GREGORY does a quick jogging trot to make his point, but DOROTHY isn't too convinced. His overlarge shorts are sliding below his knees and he has to hitch them up as they walk. He knows it's getting near now-or-never time date-wise. And he's out of puff all over again.

DOROTHY   Thanks for the practice.

She sounded and looked almost sympathetic just then, almost tender.

GREGORY   No sweat. (*He gets the joke on himself before she does. He looks down at his own dishevelment.*) Well, *lots* of sweat actually, but no sweat if you get my meaning.

DOROTHY   I'm sorry you missed lunch.

GREGORY   It's OK. Lunch means nothing to me. Some nuts, some fresh fruit.

DOROTHY   Double apple pie and custard.

GREGORY   (*sheepishly*) That kind of thing.

DOROTHY   I'm off for a shower.

With that she moves quickly and beautifully off. We hold GREGORY in the foreground of the shot as DOROTHY walks off towards the dressing rooms, getting smaller and smaller in the shot. She doesn't look back. She's not the type. GREGORY is perplexed and angry with himself. He is mouthing obscenities to himself, clenching his fists. He would like to punch himself on the mouth but it would only hurt his hand. DOROTHY is very far away now.

Then with amazing resolve, he hitches up his shorts and sprints off after her.

She is almost at the steps and GREGORY is closing fast.

55   Ext. Dressing Room Steps. Day.   55

DOROTHY is climbing the steps as GREGORY rockets into the shot and hails her. She stops and turns round. He emergency-stops himself to a halt two or three steps below her. From inside the school we hear the sound of some young musicians practising in one of the adjacent gyms. As the scene goes on they repeat over and over again a strong rhythmic rock beat. By the end of the scene they have their song properly under way.

GREGORY   (*breathless but resolute*) Dorothy! I just wanted to say – any time. For more practice, any time.

DOROTHY   Right, ta.

GREGORY   Also, would you like to come out with me?

DOROTHY   OK.

GREGORY can't quite take it in so quickly.

GREGORY   I mean, I mean on a, a kind of *date*?

DOROTHY   I said OK.

It's still not making sense to GREGORY. Is she fooling? What's going on?

GREGORY   Oh come on, stop fooling around. I mean a real.

DOROTHY   (*gets teasingly exasperated*) If you're gonna argue about it, forget it.

GREGORY   No! No! Fine. When?

DOROTHY   Tonight. Half-past seven at the clock in the Plaza.

GREGORY goes on looking happy and bemused and doesn't say anything. He just nods his head. DOROTHY gives him a quick, almost motherly smile, and vanishes inside. GREGORY is left alone on the steps with the sound of the music growing in the background. The group are well into their love song now, and it fits GREGORY's feelings perfectly. The music seems to help him to gather himself together, and he trots off to the boys' dressing rooms.

56   Int. Dressing Room.   56

DOROTHY is taking a towel out of her bag. There is a knock on the door.

DOROTHY   Yeah?

GREGORY   I . . . I . . . I just wanted to check.

DOROTHY   Yeah?

GREGORY   Tonight.

DOROTHY   Tonight.

GREGORY   Yes. Half-seven?

DOROTHY   Half-past seven.

GREGORY   And you'll be there?

DOROTHY   I'll be there.

GREGORY   And I'll be there.

DOROTHY   Uh-huh.

GREGORY   At the clock.

DOROTHY   At the clock.

GREGORY leaves.

PHIL MENZIES is heading for the dressing rooms. His office is in there somewhere amongst the hoola-hoops and the bean bags and the medicine balls and the box full of bars of carbolic soap. When he sees GREGORY vanishing into the place, however, he changes his mind. There's never enough distance between GREGORY and himself for PHIL's liking.

With a thoughtful rub of his moustache he takes himself off into the dressing rooms.

Inside, PHIL finds DOROTHY still in her strip. We can hear that she has the shower running already.

> DOROTHY Yeah. What is it?

PHIL comes in.

> PHIL Has that boy been bothering you?

> DOROTHY No. He's harmless.

> PHIL How's the training been going?

> DOROTHY I was practising some turns on the ball. I'm not too happy with it. I think I'm using my feet too much.

PHIL's eyes light up. DOROTHY's remark shows rare insight and feeling for the game! A kindred spirit at last! Here is somebody he can really *talk* to about football, someone who will understand, learn, utilise knowledge, score goals!

Not one grotty sweaty boy player in a thousand would have perceived that a turn on the ball doesn't need a lot of feet! PHIL is so happy he can't believe his luck; he gives anxious darting glances around the room as if some evil spirit will any moment snatch DOROTHY from him before he can impart his knowledge. PHIL prepares to blossom, he seems to grow in stature before our eyes, his voice becomes steady and authoritative. This is his moment.

> PHIL That little remark tells me a lot about you, sweetheart. (*DOROTHY gives PHIL all her attention.*) When you trap a ball, what you've got to do first and foremost is to kill that ball's *energy*, you've got to *tame* it! (*DOROTHY gives a kind of 'yes coach' nod.*) Now what do you use to kill a ball's energy?

> DOROTHY My feet?

PHIL   And what else?

DOROTHY   My chest?

PHIL   And?

DOROTHY shakes her head shortly and sharply. They don't notice the steam creeping from the shower room.

PHIL   (*triumphantly*) This! (*Hey presto, he places a hand on DOROTHY's bottom. Now the dramatic revelation is over, he can get down to explanation.*) Your Gluteus Maximus Trap, my dear. Now this is what you do. Right. You've got a high ball and a fast ball, but it's behind you. (*He mimes dramatically, pointing out this high, fast ball on the distant horizon.*) And you want to trap it and turn. So you let that ball bounce once, kill the momentum, then – and this is what foxes them – *reverse* up to the ball. (*He is crouching down now and walking backwards.*) Catch it on the bounce with your fleshy part. Drop down low on it and there it is. (*A dramatic pause and then the coup de grace.*) But you don't waste time. You're up on your feet. You turn. Steady – and it's yours.

There's no doubt about it, DOROTHY is impressed. She's smiling and nodding enthusiastically.

DOROTHY   Jesu bambino! That's really nifty!

PHIL allows himself this moment of admiration, then on with the work.

PHIL   Right – you try it, and I'll walk you through it. Ready? (*PHIL comes close to DOROTHY and takes her through the moves, like a ballet dancer guiding his partner.*) Reverse . . . down . . . trap . . . up . . . turn . . . steady . . . kick.

DOROTHY gets into the way of it with ease.

>DOROTHY Reverse. Down. Trap. Up. Turn. Steady.
>and PHIL Kick. Reverse. Down. Trap. Up. Turn.
>Steady. Kick.

>PHIL Reverse. Down. Trap. Up. Turn. Steady.
>Kick. Reverse. Down. Trap. Up.

We close the scene as they continue this almost ballet-like movement, with DOROTHY's voice joining in the gentle, rhythmic enunciation of the moves. It gets to look more and more like a dance because they go from the end of the sequence of moves straight to the beginning again without a break, one sequence with PHIL leading and the next with DOROTHY leading.

The thick steam curling from the shower room and creeping across the floor only makes the whole thing look more like a Fred Astaire and Ginger Rogers movie.

57 Int. Gregory's House. Day.   57

GREGORY is in the bath at home, preparing for the big date.

The scene opens outside the bathroom. MADELINE is leaning close to the door, listening to GREGORY splashing and singing. MADELINE shouts through the closed door to him.

>MADELINE Remember, do your neck.

>GREGORY Yeah.

>MADELINE And under your arms.

GREGORY shouts out to her, with a hint of mildly-tried patience in his voice.

>GREGORY Yeah, yeah, everything's under control.

MADELINE is blow-drying and combing GREGORY's hair at the mirror. She is happy to be fussing over him and he is wearing the contented, half-drowsy expression of someone being deliciously pampered.

GREGORY   Think I should tell her some jokes?

MADELINE   Maybe.

After a pause.

GREGORY   D'you know any jokes?

MADELINE   Don't tell her the one about Batman and Superwoman.

GREGORY catches her eye in the mirror and starts to giggle. The giggle turns into a full-blown, downright filthy laugh, as the remembrance of the joke takes full effect on him. MADELINE is much more under control and just giggles quietly. She eventually checks him and makes him sit still in the chair again, but we sense that she is chastising him for the thoughts going through his head as much as for his fidgeting. He calms down, although he breaks out into the odd chuckle as the coiffing continues.

MADELINE   Sit still.

For lewd-thinking, self-satisfied, pampered, date-going GREGORY, the trials of life seem to be over, or at least well under control. He plays the drums.

59   Int. Plaza. Evening.   59

GREGORY is just below the massive clock. It reads 7.30. He is waiting, and the tenseness and anticipation show on his face. He has lost his boyish cockiness of the previous scene. If he smoked he would be pulling tensely on a cigarette right now.

His thoughts can be guessed from the anxious set of his face: how should he open the conversation? How quickly should he try to put the evening onto a sexual footing? How do you get *that* under way? Has he overdone it with his father's aftershave? When you take into account that GREGORY doesn't yet shave, the answer must be a disconcerting 'Yes'.

One thing is OK at least. STEVE's jet-setter, private-eye, pop-singer white jacket feels good! He must have off-loaded at least three tons of doughnuts and assorted teacakes on the school population to afford this little number. From the outside the jacket might just be a teeny size-and-a-half too big for GREGORY, but from the inside it makes him feel like Bryan Ferry going on a date.

> GREGORY (*to himself*) Hi there! Oh, hi there.

The clock now reads 7.44. We hear the sound of light footsteps before we see anyone. So does GREGORY. Alert, he pulls himself to attention, and then decides it might be better to try the cool look. He attempts to casually absorb himself in a pair of shoes in a shop window, so that he can greet her with suave surprise.

The footsteps get closer and stop beside him. He swings his head round elegantly from the so-absorbing window. He sees CAROL. By now his nice-guy smile is well under way and it's too late to stop it.

> CAROL Hi, Gregory.

> GREGORY (*brightly and casually*) Hello Carol.

> CAROL Waiting for Dorothy?

> GREGORY (*still with the smile*) Yes.

> CAROL She's not coming.

CAROL deals her blow quickly, either out of kindness or a sadistic sense of timing.

GREGORY still has that damned smile on his face. It is

beginning to harden and lose the slight resemblance it had to a real smile in the first place. But GREGORY can't get rid of it. He can't trust his confused feelings to come up with a suitable replacement for it, at least not one that he would like CAROL to witness.

So the smile sits there and gets very tarnished-looking.

> GREGORY Many thanks. (*He walks off in the wrong direction.*) Wrong way.

> CAROL Something turned up, to do with her football I think. (*She gives GREGORY's appearance a long scrutiny.*) Is that Steve's jacket?

> GREGORY No. No. Steve's has got a stain – there – there's no stain. Eh, thanks for the word about Dorothy.

CAROL is not sure whether she believes him.

> CAROL Och, it's OK. Couldn't just leave you here all night. What will you do now?

GREGORY looks at CAROL. She's a nice-looking girl with big open eyes and glowing cheeks. Her lips are parted and she is ever-so-slightly breathless.

> GREGORY Fancy a walk?

> CAROL Where?

GREGORY senses the challenge in this innocent question. If he can come up with the goods, deliver an exotic delight or two, then he might be fit to walk up the road with.

> GREGORY We could go up to the Sports Centre.

GREGORY knows this sounds pretty tame. CAROL looks pretty unmoved by the idea. It's hard work going on dates, even when the wrong girl turns up!

> CAROL No. I'm pretty hungry, you know.

> GREGORY We can go up to Capaldi's, and I'll buy you
> some chips.

> CAROL Well, OK. I'm going that way anyway.

It's all a bit remote from 'dancing cheek to cheek'. But to
GREGORY's crude thinking, the chips seem to have swung
the evening back in his favour for a while.

60   Ext. Street. Evening.   60

> CAROL Gregory, hold on a minute.

She dodges into a phone box. Up until now CAROL has been
dressed in a straightforward kind of way, with casual slacks
and practical, fashionable shoes. GREGORY is astonished to
witness a rapid transformation. From her shoulderbag she
takes out black lipstick, mirror and afro-comb. She paints her
lips quickly and expertly in a black Cupid's bow, combs out
her tidy hair, changes her shoes for horrific white winkle-
picker stilettos, unzips her slacks and steps out of them to
reveal black stretch skin tights underneath. She transforms
herself instantly from wholesome college girl to Punk Witch.
She is too businesslike for it to be any kind of performance
for GREGORY's sake. As she applies the final black touches of
make-up to her eyes, she heaves a deep sigh.

> CAROL Well, I feel like a human being again.

She marches off, leaving GREGORY a little agog. He watches
her for a second.

> GREGORY Look, I've really got to go home. I really
> enjoyed the walk. You go that way, right, and
> I'll go this way. See you.

CAROL grabs his arm.

> CAROL Hold it, Gregory. I thought we were going for
> chips?

GREGORY   Chips? OK. There you are – fifty pence.
           You'll get loads of them with that. Bye.

CAROL grabs his arm again.

CAROL   Don't be stupid. Come on, you're worse than
         my Dad, and he's old – at least he's got an
         excuse for being a prick.

GREGORY   OK, OK. Put your coat on.

CAROL   Oh, no. Look, come on Gregory. All I'm
         asking for is a walk up to the chip shop. I've
         got a date. I'm going away. I've just got a
         funny feeling that something nice might
         happen up there, so come on.

GREGORY   OK. Walk ahead.

CAROL   Come on Gregory, hurry up. We haven't got
         all night.

61 Ext. Chip Shop. Evening.   61

There's the sense of more activity up this end of town. A few
more YOUNG PEOPLE are around, going to and from the café
and generally hanging about. GREGORY and CAROL are
perched on the back of a concrete bench, nibbling at their chips.

CAROL   D'you really fancy Dorothy?

GREGORY   Yeah.

CAROL   Can you drive?

GREGORY   No, but it runs in the family. Why?

CAROL   Oh, it's just that Ricky Swift has got a car.
         Dorothy knows him. He's up at the Physical
         Ed. College.

GREGORY tries to bring some harsh realism into this picture
of Ricky.

GREGORY Must be quite old then, eh?

CAROL He's nearly nineteen.

GREGORY takes it all on the chin.

GREGORY Nineteen. Has he got any hair left? Ricky
Swift! Sounds like something out of a comic!
Does he fly through the air like Batman?

The collection of self-conjured images is too much for
GREGORY. A bald-headed Batman in a college blazer. He
retreats into laughter.

CAROL affects an air of non-amusement at GREGORY's
childish behaviour, but it's doing *him* the world of good. He
knows by some instinct that ridicule is a good first line of
defence against the Carols and the Rickys of life. The lessons
are coming thick and fast tonight.

GREGORY (*in a mock cartoon-type voice*) Quick Dorothy,
to the Rickmobile.

CAROL OK, calm down, don't wet yourself.

And GREGORY does calm down. In an instant the hysteria
has been washed away, and a sober-faced GREGORY gets on
with his chips. This makes CAROL feel much more at ease.

CAROL Well, lover boy, I'm off. (*She hails another girl
passing on her way to the chippy, no doubt.*)
Hey, Margo, here's Gregory. (*MARGO
approaches them dutifully.*) Dorothy stood
him up, so he's buying everybody chips and
making jokes. (*CAROL stands up to go.*) Have
fun, Gregory. You can tell me all about it
tomorrow. (*CAROL looks in GREGORY's chip
bag, at the pickled onion.*) By the way, pickled
onions and dates don't mix. You might have
to do some kissing later on. Bye.

Then she leaves. GREGORY and MARGO are left alone.

She takes the initiative.

> MARGO Well, I'll buy my own chips. You keep telling
> the jokes.

So GREGORY trots after Lady Number Two. Whether he
knows it or not, he's getting a rare education tonight.
MARGO is a different kettle of mermaid from CAROL. For a
start she is a lot more outwardly 'emancipated' or 'liberated'
or whatever the current word is. Not that the other girls in
the movie aren't, it's just that MARGO is more obviously so,
and she can put it into words.

GREGORY waits outside the chip shop until MARGO comes
out with her bag. She seems already to be in command as she
directs him to wait for her while she goes into a nearby
phone box and makes a quick call. GREGORY gets to hold her
chips while she is inside. We stay outside with GREGORY as
he politely keeps the chips warm inside Steve's jacket. He
sees ANDY and CHARLIE.

> ANDY What's going on?

> GREGORY I don't know. I think Margo's after me. I get
> that feeling.

> ANDY It's a good night for it. Are you taking her up
> to the Country Park?

> GREGORY Don't know. Do you think I should?

> ANDY Aye.

> GREGORY Yeah.

62 Ext. Telephone Box. Evening. 62

SUSAN leans against the telephone box. The 'phone rings.
SUSAN opens the door and goes in. She picks up the 'phone.

MARGO is on the 'phone. She hangs up the receiver and walks out.

GREGORY sees MARGO finishing her call and starts to drift down the road away from the box. When MARGO comes out she calls him back and indicates that they are going the other way. He shrugs his shoulders and follows her.

All of this happens without perceptible dialogue on the soundtrack. Perhaps even some music over the barely heard natural sounds.

As they leave, ANDY turns to CHARLIE.

> ANDY It's a fine night for it, eh? You know there's definitely something in the air tonight, Charlie. Something in the atmosphere.

So GREGORY and MARGO are on the move. Past the kiddies' football field with a noisy game in progress, up towards the villa-type houses with the open-plan gardens and the gawky adolescent trees supported by adult-looking stakes.

> MARGO Relax.

> GREGORY Where are we going?

> MARGO Relax. Enjoy it.

> GREGORY I am. Ah well.

GREGORY puts his arm round MARGO.

> MARGO What are you up to?

GREGORY takes his arm away, and holds up his hands.

> GREGORY Nothing, nothing. Look, what's going on? Where are we going? Where are you and I going?

> MARGO I told you to relax. You can't enjoy yourself if you don't relax.

GREGORY I'm just a bit emotional tonight. OK?

MARGO That's OK. It's fine. Nothing wrong with a
bit of emotion – come on.

64   Ext. Bollards. Evening.   64

At first glance SUSAN looks as if she has seen too many
Bacall/Dietrich movies on TV. She wears a loose-fitting white
raincoat, belt tied at the waist, and a beret. She is the kind of
girl who suits berets. She hasn't gone for the sultry, pulled-
down-over-one-eye look with the beret. With her individual
sense of style she has it set well back on her head. This only
adds to her open attractiveness. She wears make-up, but not
so much that it detracts from her youthful kind of beauty.
The glowing cheeks and bright eyes are there under the
perfect degree of Revlon Creme Blush and Max Factor Hazy
Blue. It might be helped by the costume, but she has a strong
air about her, a kind of modest self-assertiveness.

TOP SECRET! Don't tell GREGORY, but the meeting is a
put-up job, as a result of MARGO's phone call earlier. In the
hour since he left home tonight GREGORY has been the pawn
in more female ruses than you could shake a stick at. But this
one at least is on the up and up. SUSAN rather fancies him.
But don't tell him yet, nor the audience.

MARGO and GREGORY meet SUSAN.

SUSAN Hello Gregory. What are you up to?

He gestures with his hand and blows out through his mouth,
then shrugs.

MARGO We're just cruising.

SUSAN You're all dressed up – anywhere to go?

MARGO I've got somewhere to go. See you tomorrow,
Susan.

MARGO leaves them.

SUSAN   I believe you're short of a date.

GREGORY   Well, there was a bit of a mix-up earlier on.
It's OK.

SUSAN   Would you like to spend some time with me?
On a kind of date?

GREGORY laughs.

GREGORY   Look, I'm not very sure what's going on. Is
there some kind of joke? All this, with Carol
and Margo and . . . It's a joke, isn't it?

SUSAN   Not a joke. It's just the way girls work. They
help each other.

GREGORY   It's Dorothy.

SUSAN   Dorothy is a good sport. Anyway, how about
it? You and me – what do you say? (*GREGORY
is overcome with embarrassment.*) Think about
it. Sit down over there and think about it.

GREGORY sits for a few moments, thinking.

GREGORY   OK. A kind of date. Do we start right away?

SUSAN   Yeah. We'll go to the Country Park. It's too
nice an evening to sit in a bar.

GREGORY   Yeah. Far too nice.

65   Ext. Country Park. Evening.   65

GREGORY and SUSAN are both at their ease away from the
bright lights, and they can act their age again. The Country
Park is exactly that: a one-time country estate which has
mated itself with the New Town. So now it has nature trails
and picnic areas, and the old-time stables are now the Golf
Club House. For most people around these parts it does an
excellent job as 'the countryside'. And what's wrong with a
fancy estate having seventy thousand lairds instead of one?

They are strolling up a grassy hill with, for once, mature trees scattered here and there. The evening's adventure has really brought them close, a bond between them. This is right up SUSAN's alley. GREGORY is not quite on her wavelength yet, but give him a chance and a little nudge now and then from SUSAN and he'll catch up.

> SUSAN What . . . what we'll do is, we'll just walk and talk. And we don't even need to talk that much either. We'll just see how it goes.

> GREGORY Fine.

> SUSAN I hope you don't think I do this kind of thing all the time.

> GREGORY Huh – no. Can we whistle too?

> SUSAN Yes, we can whistle too.

> GREGORY Good. (*They continue to talk, whistling.*) If we were going for a drink . . .

> SUSAN Uh-huh?

> GREGORY What would you have to drink?

> SUSAN Eh, a Bacardi and Coke – with ice.

> GREGORY Same here. With ice.

ANDY and CHARLIE see GREGORY and SUSAN.

> ANDY There's definitely something in the air tonight, Charlie. That's three women in a row he's had.

Further on in their walk:

> SUSAN I like your jacket.

> GREGORY I like your skirt.

> SUSAN I like your shirt.

> GREGORY I like your beret.

SUSAN Thank you.

GREGORY Want to swop? Now this is really good. I'm enjoying myself.

SUSAN Good. I'm glad we bumped into each other.

GREGORY Do you want to dance? (*He lays down on the ground.*) It's really good. You just lie flat down and dance. I'll show you what I mean – I'll, I'll start it off and you just join in when you feel confident enough.

SUSAN OK.

He starts 'dancing' – mostly with his arms.

GREGORY Just dance.

SUSAN OK.

GREGORY I'll tell you something. And not a lot of people know this.

SUSAN Uh-huh?

GREGORY We are clinging to a surface of this planet while it spins through space at a thousand miles an hour held only by the mystery force called gravity.

SUSAN Wow.

GREGORY A lot of people panic when you tell them that, and they just fall off.

SUSAN Oh.

GREGORY But I can see you're not falling off. That means you've got the hang of it. That means that you have got . . .

SUSAN Natural ability?

SUSAN bends herself sideways. We cut to a shot of her point of view, taken with the camera tilted so that GREGORY lying down appears vertical in the frame. He does indeed look as if he is clinging to some massive spinning wall, like at the fairground. He looks at SUSAN/THE CAMERA and sums up his feat.

GREGORY Yeah. A thousand miles an hour, eh?

SUSAN Why are boys obsessed with numbers?

GREGORY No, I'm not.

SUSAN You are!

GREGORY Don't stop to answer or you'll fall off.

ERIC comes up to them. ERIC, the photographer, is carrying his fancy Japanese camera but this time it is wearing a fantastic telephoto lens, about eighteen inches long and as thick as a milk bottle. ERIC is laden down with other bits and pieces – an accessory bag and a folded-up tripod. If SUSAN can hold on for a moment ERIC will prove her point about numbers.

ERIC What are you two up to?

This query seems to be directed at only GREGORY.

GREGORY Well, what are *you* up to?

ERIC tries to get the message across to GREGORY without SUSAN catching on. He is heading back down to the Nurses' Hostel, this time loaded down with exactly the right equipment for the photograph of the century. He will sit up all night if necessary. He tries to tell GREGORY all of this by mime and winks and insinuation, and nods of the head in the general direction of the Hostel.

ERIC I'm going down to the Hospital to do the exposure test, the flesh-tone experiment.

GREGORY catches on at last, and sits up with interest.

GREGORY Oh yeah, the flesh-tone *experiment*, of course. Have you got the right equipment?

GREGORY gives SUSAN the odd wary glance. So does ERIC.

> ERIC   Of course. Four-hundred-millimetre lens.
> It opens up to two point eight, which with
> seven-hundred-foot candles at, say, a
> hundred yards, and a film-speed of three
> hundred and sixty and a force processing of
> about one point five stops.

> SUSAN   Do you like numbers, Eric?

> ERIC   Numbers make the world go round.

> GREGORY   How many, um, elephants will you give it
> tonight?

> SUSAN   Elephants?

> ERIC   We can't have any time exposures. That
> would ruin the image definition.

> GREGORY   Don't want to ruin the image definition, eh?

> ERIC   Right. So that means a fast shutter. Say, at the
> outside, one hundred and twenty-fifth of an
> elephant?

> GREGORY   Sounds fine.

> SUSAN   Fine.

> ERIC   Are you coming?

> GREGORY   No. I'd be quite interested in the results
> though.

ERIC gets his gear together and starts off down the hill.

> ERIC   Want to make an advance order for some
> eight-by-tens?

GREGORY shouts after him.

> GREGORY   Yeah, put me down for six . . . (*He glances at*
> *SUSAN. She seems to enjoy the nonsense of it.*)
> No, make it half a dozen!

SUSAN and GREGORY are alone again. They look at each other openly and we sense that the little flame has been lit at last. They both seem happy in the knowledge that something is under way between them, something nice, but at this stage they don't need too many words. They are calm, sitting close to each other, touching.

> SUSAN Listen, I want to tell you something. D'you know when you sneeze it comes right down your nose at a hundred miles per hour?

> GREGORY Really?

> SUSAN Mm. Just like that.

> GREGORY One more number: eleven, home by, I've got to be.

> SUSAN OK Mister Spaceman, I'll walk you home.

The evening light is fading as they set off, holding each other closely. GREGORY teases her.

> GREGORY Really?

> SUSAN Uh-huh.

> GREGORY I don't want to put you to any trouble.

> SUSAN It's OK.

> GREGORY If you just want to walk me to the bridge, that's fine.

> SUSAN All the way home. I don't mind.

> GREGORY OK. I'll do the same for you sometime.

> SUSAN Good.

She lets him chatter on as they take the path back to town. She amuses herself by humming a tune and doing a few little dance steps as she hangs onto his arm, gentle soft-shoe-shuffle steps. It's her little victory dance. She bullies GREGORY into joining in.

SUSAN and GREGORY are in the half-shadows, kissing. In between the kisses they talk. When GREGORY gets short on conversation he simply says a number, and it always stimulates another kiss from SUSAN. She tries it out as well and gets the same treatment from GREGORY. We start the scene as they are relaxing after a kiss, taking a breath and holding each other very close.

> SUSAN   That's better. You've stopped kissing me like I was your auntie. Nobody's looking.

They kiss again.

> GREGORY   What's my Auntie gonna say when I kiss her at Christmas?

They kiss again.

> SUSAN   Say something.

> GREGORY   Three hundred and forty-two.

She reaches to him and kisses him.

> SUSAN   A million and nine.

She gets a kiss for that.

> GREGORY   How come you know all the good numbers? (*They kiss.*) Thanks for seeing me home. (*She kisses him.*) When can I see you again?

A little kiss.

> SUSAN   Tomorrow. History. Ten thirty.

A bigger kiss.

> GREGORY   I want a date.

A longer kiss.

> SUSAN   OK Mister Spaceman. Twelve thirty. Room 17 tomorrow. We'll talk about it.

He kisses her.

GREGORY Ten four.

One last kiss.

SUSAN Goodnight Mister Spaceman.

A peck on the cheek.

GREGORY Three hundred and seventy-five. Five
thousand, six hundred and seventy-two.

67 Int. Gregory's House. Night. 67

We start off in MADELINE's bedroom. The room is in
darkness. She puts on the bed-lamp and we see her sneaking
out of bed. She makes her way quietly to Gregory's room. It
is in darkness as she creeps in and switches on the bed-lamp.
We find GREGORY not asleep but lying wide awake in bed
with his hands folded under his head. He is smiling. A smile
with a bit of bemusement in it, and a lot of happiness.
MADELINE crawls onto his bed and squats beside him. They
talk in low voices.

MADELINE How did it go? Are you gonna see her again?

GREGORY Who? Dorothy?

MADELINE Who else?

GREGORY (*mysteriously*) Well – maybe Susan, for
instance.

MADELINE is too eager for news to stand for this coy stuff.
She grabs him by the pyjama collar and starts banging his
head off the pillow.

MADELINE Tell me, or I'll hurt you. Tell me.

GREGORY OK, OK. Dorothy didn't turn up. But I met
Carol and then Margo and then *Susan*. She's
lovely. We went into the park. I think she

likes me. I'll see her tomorrow.

MADELINE Did you kiss her?

GREGORY No. Maybe tomorrow.

MADELINE forgets to whisper.

MADELINE You liar! I saw you! You kissed her about
fifty times!

GREGORY tries to quieten her.

GREGORY Shush! You'll wake the mater and pater.

MADELINE calms down and becomes more affectionate.

MADELINE I better kiss you too then. [*She gives him a
cross between an auntie kiss and a Susan kiss.*]
It's hard work being in love, eh? Especially
when you don't know which girl it is.

GREGORY Yeah, I'll work on it.

MADELINE Who's going to be Gregory's girl?

GREGORY You are!

MADELINE pulls the pillow from under his head and shoves
it over his face. Then she gives it a friendly thump just where
she reckons his face must be. She jumps off the bed and
disappears back to her own. GREGORY makes himself
comfortable again and lies back, settled for sleep. He
stretches over and puts out the light.

After the click of the light switch we hold on the blackness
for a moment or two as the END TITLE MUSIC starts. It might
even be a song. Then once the music is under way we cut to
our end scene.

68   Ext. Motorway Verge. Twilight.   68

ANDY and CHARLIE are here. ANDY is positioned at the
roadside. He holds a piece of card with the word 'CARACUS'

written on it. He looks down the empty roadway, with a worn look on his face. They have obviously been hanging around for a long time, most of the long summer evening probably.

CHARLIE is sitting on the nearside barrier, back from the road. He looks at ANDY. After a short while, he speaks.

> CHARLIE Come on Andy, let's go home. That's not the way to spell Caracas anyway.
>
> ANDY What? What d'you mean?
>
> CHARLIE Caracas is spelt with an 'a' – c, a, s – not c, u, s.
>
> ANDY Well, why didn't you tell me that before? Could you not have told me that four hours ago? We're standing here, waiting, frustrated.
>
> CHARLIE Well, let's go home. Come on, we can start again tomorrow. There are some nice girls in the third year. They always go for the older guys. At least the nice ones do. There's even a couple of dolls in second year. I saw them the other day at home. Do you know, they were amazing. Andy, I think everything's going to be all right.

69   Ext. Country Park. Night.   69

GREGORY might be safely and happily in bed, but there is still some life in the New Town yet.

In the late summer night enough light persists to allow us to see DOROTHY, in a solitary training session. Dressed in her tracksuit she makes her way through the Country Park. Jogging is too angular a word to describe her fluid and purposeful movement. We stay with her for a final moment or two and then we let her merge into the twilight.

The sign reads

GLASGOW	20
EDINBURGH	25
CARACUS	9,000 miles

END

Appendix

The following scenes or parts of scenes are taken from the pre-production script. They are *not* found in the final version. The pre-production script was very different from the final version, and only the main changes are recorded here.

The original opening scenes

Title Scene
A full frame-shot of the oil painting, 'The Lang Riggs, Cumbernauld', by R. Russel Macnee, painted in 1883.

The canvas shows the long narrow enclosures of land stretching down from the row of single-storey houses. The trees and fields are green, and above is a full-blown summer cumulus sky.

We superimpose our main title: GREGORY's GIRL.

When the title fades from the screen we begin a slow dissolve from the canvas to the present-day scene from exactly the same vantage point. One or two prominent features – a church steeple and a farmhouse – will anchor the two images together.

The general look of the old houses hasn't changed all that much. But above and below the thin line of houses things have happened. A trunk-road laden with heavy goods traffic appears on the middle horizon. Modern houses begin to appear in the area below 'The Lang Riggs'. The soundtrack also comes alive, with modern noises of traffic and, faintly still, the sounds of a game of football.

Almost as soon as our modern image is fixed on the screen we pan off to the right, revealing the modern New Town all around our old village. We find the football field and the match in progress. It's a casual local match, with a handful of people and kids watching.

Next Scene

The football match seems an incidental event in the previous scene, but in the following images we make our point. This town is football crazy. From every vantage point we are offered yet another football field with yet another game in progress; sometimes two or three games in the one shot, at other times a simple camera movement revealing two fields and two games in relation to each other.

We see a primary school field with a tiny-tots match in progress; a tightly bunched swarm of bodies chasing after the ball, lost somewhere in their midst. We see the town playing fields, with no less than eight games in progress.

All of these images we will hold in wide shot, showing as much of the setting of the town as the football action.

Our final football game will be the school game involving GREGORY.

Two more early scenes

New Town exterior. Near the motorway
We start on a close shot of the town sign:

MIDDLETON NEW TOWN	
GLASGOW	20 MILES
EDINBURGH	25 MILES

A bucket of water is splashed onto the sign. We cut to a wider shot to reveal a motorway maintenance gang at work on the sign and the adjoining roundabout and slip road. A gang of seven young people, dressed in their red safety waistcoats, looking suspiciously like a job creation project. They scrub down the signs and the traffic island lights and they tend the grass verges with shears and grass cutters.

A very definite flavour of the garden gnomes at work. They are all whistling, in fact. A well-known tune from a very popular Disney move. They work well together, and they have developed elaborate harmonies in their whistling.

Pedestrian Bridge. Motorway

We link to the previous scene with one tracking shot along the motorway, some of the dialogue from this scene laid over it. Our track shot passes under the pedestrian bridge, and the camera tilts up to find two figures on the bridge as it passes underneath.

The figures are GREGORY and GARY.

GARY leans on the railing and all through the scene keeps some of his attention on the motorway. He carries a notebook and a little device that helps him count things. He is a traffic enumerator. He is the same age as GREGORY.

GREGORY   What's the money like?

GARY   It's not fantastic. It's not top money. I wish I got paid by the vehicle count. I can log up to fifteen hundred trucks in a day here!

GREGORY   You just add them up?

GARY   No, division as well – divide them into private vehicles and goods vehicles. (*He logs in a truck or two.*) I'm getting married.

GREGORY is incredulous.

GREGORY   Married? Come on, you're joking.

GARY   Nup. We're having a baby. Me and Fiona.

GREGORY   Jesus!

GARY   Christ.

GREGORY   When did it . . . all start?

GARY   Remember Gordon's party? (*GREGORY nods.*) Well, it was then (*GREGORY keeps nodding*) or the night before (*GREGORY stops nodding*) or the night after. (*GARY gives GREGORY a straight look.*) It's a terrible thing, sex. I hope you're being a good boy, Gregory.

GREGORY   Yeah, I'm being a good boy . . .

An awkwardness has crept in between them. GREGORY
makes to move off.

A scene before Gregory arrives at school

The next voice that greets GREGORY belongs to MR WYLIE.

MR WYLIE   Morning Gregory.

MR WYLIE is a retired gent, wearing a pair of binoculars
around his neck, smiling.

MR WYLIE   Late again?

GREGORY   No, no. I was up late doing some astronomy,
checking out some heavenly bodies. I get
time off in the morning.

MR WYLIE   You're an awful liar Gregory.

GREGORY gives him a smile. He nods in the direction of the
binoculars.

GREGORY   Do these things work in the dark?

MR WYLIE   Oh yes, they most certainly do. You name it,
and they bring it closer, day or night . . .

GREGORY   (*more interested than he admits*) What kind of
things?

MR WYLIE   Dogs? Pussy cats? All forms of wildlife.

Continuation of scene 10

GREGORY   You're a terrible liar, Mr Wylie.

They both give a laugh. By now they are approaching the bus
stop. GREGORY joins the small queue, made up of young
mums and kiddies and push-chairs.

MR WYLIE   What's the idea? School's just up the road.

A bus is approaching. GREGORY is giving it all of his
attention as he replies to MR WYLIE.

GREGORY Big rush now.

The bus has stopped. Something about it doesn't satisfy GREGORY. He looks at his watch, then gives an anxious look up the road. He doesn't make any move to get on the bus.

MR WYLIE watches all this curiously. Then he seems to give up trying to figure it out. The bus moves off, and MR WYLIE makes to walk off up the road.

MR WYLIE Nice talking to you, Gregory. You don't get a lot of male conversation around here. See you around.

Only one lady has remained at the bus stop in front of GREGORY. She has a baby strapped to her back in a papoose. GREGORY makes a friendly face at it.

We might just have a clue for GREGORY's behaviour at the bus stop. The next bus is being driven by a very attractive young woman. The type that even James Bond would have gone for, because she doesn't 'drive like a woman', one of his regular complaints about females.

As soon as we see her, the music starts. She has an open quality about her face, bordering on a constant smile, and the sun catching her hair and eyes adds to the effect.

She steers her bus towards the waiting GREGORY. We film the whole scene from aboard the bus, so that we see his face light up as she approaches the stop. We see him almost push the mother and the papoose out of the way in his eagerness to offer his fare to her. He smiles and she smiles. He goes on smiling as they move off, and he sits himself down in the front-row seat, opposite her.

The music continues throughout the scene, as we intercut from GREGORY's face to hers. He only has one disconcerting moment during the short journey. As the bus passes the Nurses' Hostel a group of nurses are leaving the building. GREGORY's attention is caught between his dream driver and the nurses, in a few seconds of confusion.

The dream bus draws up and GREGORY gets out. We hold on him for a moment as he watches the bus drive off.

Then he comes back to reality. The music fades off as well, as if it is travelling off with the bus, as if *she* indeed creates the music and has it with her always.

Anyway, GREGORY is all alone at the side of the road, and late for school as usual. He hurries off.

Near scene 44

An excited GREGORY is fixing his hair in the empty boys' toilet. He's busy at the mirror with comb and dabs of water. The school bell rings and he leaves the toilet to make his way to his rendezvous in Room 9. Hordes of young people are spilling out of the classrooms for the break. This gives us the opportunity again to leave GREGORY and his concerns for a bit and let one or two other young people inhabit the film. GREGORY's story is after all only one from a possible two thousand in the school, and the film should keep a sense of this. A kind of rhythm between the slightly distanced observation of lives in general and the intense concentration on GREGORY. Anyway, GREGORY is the kind of guy you need a break from. So we find LISA and PETE in amongst the throng. They are leaning against a wall in the main thoroughfare. GREGORY passes on his way up to Room 9, and we stay with them.

They are feeding each other crisps from a packet each, so that they never eat from their own packet. We find them well into a conversation.

       LISA No.

They feed each other.

       PETE But I love you. I really do.

       LISA That's not the point.

More feeding.

PETE Well, when then?

LISA I don't know. Maybe in the summer.

PETE But it's dangerous to wait too long. It's unhealthy. It's bad for you. I really love you.

LISA If you love me you can wait then.

PETE Shit, I knew you would say that, you got that in a book didn't you?

We leave LISA and PETE and find EDDIE and MIKE.

We catch a snatch of conversation between EDDIE and MIKE.

EDDIE We won't get married 'til next summer. I want to get the exams out of the way first, get my A-level Logic under my belt. Mary feels the same way.

MIKE Very sound reasoning.

We leave EDDIE and MIKE.

And we find a more furtive, and younger, pair, JANICE and CHRISTINE.

JANICE We'll meet them up at the cemetery at eight – and bring something warm, and don't bring Isabel.

Next, in a quieter corridor we find a wandering PHIL MENZIES. Ahead of him we see the curvaceous back view of MISS WELCH. PHIL hitches his tracksuit out from the cheeks of his bottom and, in the absence of a tie, straightens his whistle. Then he quickens his pace and we leave him as he accelerates towards her.

Part of scenes 63–64

MARGO has a good-hearted laugh at GREGORY's outburst. So good-hearted that he has to laugh himself. It releases the last of his tension.

MARGO You're really *young*!

GREGORY Same age as you.

MARGO No. Girls mature quicker. You're still a wee boy.

GREGORY I'm just a bit emotional.

MARGO I know what the secret is, girls *help* each other more. They support each other, makes them stronger.

GREGORY Thanks for the tip. I'll pass it on.

MARGO forces her point.

MARGO If you were going to stand a girl up on a date, you wouldn't send Pete out to give her the news, would you?

The thought of randy PETE near *any* girl he fancies brings the point home to GREGORY.

GREGORY Very fair point. (*He gives it some thought.*) Anyway, I can join the gang?

MARGO (*laughing*) That's what *all* fellas are trying to do. That's why they love us. They want to get into the gang!

GREGORY Why are you telling *me* all your secrets?

MARGO Because you're a mug, and they won't do you any good.

GREGORY Maybe I'll change. (*MARGO shakes her head firmly, as if to say 'not possible'.*) Maybe I'll tell the other guys.

MARGO Nobody listens to a mug.

Despite the seeming insults, GREGORY is really warming to this conversation. The privilege of it all is dawning on him.

He is also becoming aware of the easefulness between himself and MARGO. So, as if to prove that he really is a mug, he tries to get seductive. He manages to do it with a pinch of style, however.

GREGORY slips an arm around MARGO's waist.

> GREGORY There's something else I wonder if you can help me with.

MARGO casts a wary eye on the armhold.

> MARGO Oh yeah?

> GREGORY Yeah. I feel that I can talk to you. I feel that I could get really close to you, really intimate.

MARGO plays him along, just for the fun of it. She is a warm girl, capable of being flirtatious, and so she knows all the routines. She leans her head back on his shoulder and gazes at him with mock passion.

> MARGO Oh yeah?

GREGORY is too eager to catch any of the irony in her act.

> GREGORY D'you want to go through the Country Park?

MARGO brings her act to a climax.

> MARGO Oh! The Country Park! The Country Park! Those words that boil my blood and turn me to JELLY!

With the word 'JELLY!' she collapses into GREGORY's arms and makes herself completely limp. Half-stumbling, he supports her as she raves on, her arms hanging loosely, her heels dragging on the ground.

> MARGO How long sir, have I waited for these words of passion from you! Be gentle with me! Take me! But remember, I have eaten of the pickled onion!

MARGO refuses to ease GREGORY of the burden. He struggles on with her full weight, and by now he's getting self-conscious and is casting anxious glances up and down the street.

GREGORY OK, Margo, very funny, ha ha.

MARGO keeps up her 'passionate maiden' voice.

MARGO Now do you believe you're a mug?

GREGORY Yes, yes, yes, I'm a mug, and I can't drive, and you're the tops.

MARGO relents and stands up. They both fix their clothing. Then MARGO gets a little mischievous again. She whispers closely in his ear.

MARGO Now, what was all that about the Country Park?

GREGORY admits defeat and laughs. They continue walking. In fact Margo hurries him along, as if they've got an appointment somewhere.

And very soon they do meet someone. SUSAN is coming down the road towards them, past the new church that looks like a huge concrete circus tent, with a stainless-steel cross on the top. We have seen SUSAN before in the film. She was the girl scampering up the stairs late that very first morning. We have seen her briefly and silently in the dining hall and in the class. And we saw ALAN trying to chat her up in the playground. She has been a consciously insistent presence.

MARGO (*with a hint of affected surprise*) Oh, hello Susan!

SUSAN and MARGO now go into a routine. It's the one that boys (and grown men) usually do about being detectives; talking in American accents and saying things like 'who's de broad' and 'don't leave town without you should let me know', etc.

SUSAN pulls her collar up, lowers her eyes and gives a jerk of the head towards GREGORY.

> SUSAN Who's de guy?

MARGO goes straight into the act and the accent.

> MARGO Sex maniac. Picked him up at Capaldi's. I'm gonna throw de book at him. Illegal possession. (*SUSAN lifts an eyebrow.*) Pickled onions. Sexual assault.

SUSAN winces at this horrific list of felonies.

> SUSAN They'll lock him up and brick the door in.

GREGORY smiles. He quite likes the sex maniac label.

The MARGO/SUSAN routine goes on.

> SUSAN What about resistin' a breast?

> MARGO Naw, we couldn't make *that* stick with dis joker. He's got so many hands he makes an octopus look like de Venus de Milo.

> SUSAN Where d'ya get the coat, fella?

GREGORY is not up to a reply. He lowers his eyes.

> MARGO Looks ta me like Seed-cake Steve's.

> SUSAN Seed-cake Steve? The Master Baker? (*Then she looks at GREGORY.*) You're mixin' in some company, fella. Your goose is really cooked. You're in de soup up to here! (*She draws a hand sharply up to her neck.*) Turtle-neck soup.

> MARGO Give de creep a break. He's had some lousy breaks. His old man runs a grocery store. The whole family can't be clearing more than three hundred a week.

And so they drag themselves back to reality, and assume their normal voices.

MARGO What are you up to, Susan?

SUSAN Just cruising around.

MARGO Join the gang then.

The three of them walk on, past the park with the boating
pond, with the Olympic-sized swimming baths on the
skyline.

GREGORY is feeling sensitive from all his recent upsets.
He speaks to MARGO.

GREGORY Don't you want to tell Susan about how
I can't drive, and about being a mug, and
everything?

MARGO takes this opportunity to leave. Her mission for the
night accomplished.

MARGO You can tell her all about your defects
yourself. I'm off. See you tomorrow.

With a quick wink to SUSAN, she leaves them and sets off
over the grassy rise towards the baths.

GREGORY is alone with Lady Number Three.

SUSAN Well, who's going to be the leader of the
gang now? (*GREGORY shrugs his shoulders.*)
D'you want to go through the Country Park?

She is probably saying this in innocence, but it gives
GREGORY a smile.

GREGORY Yeah, that's a good idea.

SUSAN Why don't we pick up a drink on the way?

We find them at the entrance to a big modern bar-and-
lounge place. It's not dark yet but the place is brightly lit
inside and the music and crowded bar sounds are drifting
out into the open. GREGORY and SUSAN are having a
discreet, whispered conversation before going in.

GREGORY seems to be in command at this stage. He is giving SUSAN the final briefing. She looks at him respectfully.

GREGORY Right, you're having a . . .?

SUSAN Bacardi and Coke, with ice.

GREGORY Right! And I'm having a dark rum and a lager.

SUSAN Right!

GREGORY gives her a confidence-building look.

GREGORY Right! Come on!

They go into the house of evil. It's very swish and adult and a daunting place for the pair of them. If it was busier it might be a bit easier to merge into the background, but there are only couples sitting here and there; most of the punters are in the bar.

SUSAN hovers behind GREGORY as he goes to the bar and catches the BARMAN's eye. The BARMAN comes over to him and GREGORY gives him a please-be-nice smile.

GREGORY A rum and ice please, and a Bacardi and a lager and a coke.

The BARMAN, unsmiling, leans over the bar to him, and nods to GREGORY to get closer. So GREGORY leans over to him too.

BARMAN (*in a soft voice, but firmly*) Piss off. Get out.

GREGORY draws away from the BARMAN, and keeps the remains of his smile on his face.

GREGORY Thank you.

He and SUSAN smartly exit.